Philip Phillips

The New Complete Standard Singer

For Sabbath Schools, Public Worship and Special Services

Philip Phillips

The New Complete Standard Singer
For Sabbath Schools, Public Worship and Special Services

ISBN/EAN: 9783337290214

Printed in Europe, USA, Canada, Australia, Japan

Cover: Foto ©Thomas Meinert / pixelio.de

More available books at **www.hansebooks.com**

THE

NEW COMPLETE

STANDARD SINGER,

For

Sabbath Schools, Public Worship, and Special Services.

BY

PHILIP PHILLIPS,

AUTHOR OF "SINGING PILGRIM," "MUSICAL LEAVES," "NEW HYMN AND TUNE-BOOK,"
ETC., ETC., ETC.

PHILIP PHILLIPS, AUTHOR AND PUBLISHER,
805 BROADWAY, NEW YORK......56 OLD BAILEY, LONDON.

HITCHCOCK & WALDEN,
CINCINNATI, CHICAGO, AND ST. LO, IS.

REFACE.

This Book appears in answer to many solicitations, from sources which are worthy of respect and response. The plan and contents of the "Singing Pilgrim" have been so heartily endorsed both in this country and in Europe, that a kindred want seems to have been created by its use—viz., that of a Book which shall contain the *Tried* and *Standard Songs* of the Sanctuary, the Prayer Room and the Sabbath School. These pages are largely enriched by pieces that have outlived the ephemeral melodies of the day; the words and music of which have become sacred to the heart, and which repeated use will only the more endear to all who sing or hear them at home, at social or public services, abroad, or anywhere.

Besides these *Gems* (that age will only intensify in value), this book contains many New Compositions prepared not merely to add to the list of books already extant, but rather to reach and rescue human souls by the charms of the Gospel.

Mere sentiment in poetry and jingle of sound, however pleasing to the ear, have been avoided, for the sake of truth in tones, that are at once delightful and dignified.

It will be observed that this work is arranged in topical departments, a feature which will commend itself to all lovers of order. Choristers and Leaders will find this arrangement one of great convenience. As any phase of christian experience can be readily supplemented by a song, *there is always a double power in a tune expressive of the words! and this power is doubled again when the words are made to emphasize and re-echo the theme of the moment.*

Adaptation to times, circumstances and impressions is essential to the "Service of Song," and makes every note of praise an appointed Missionary of good.

To the numerous composers whose productions appear in this work, under their respective names, the Author tenders his *grateful acknowledgments.*

A few of the choicest pieces have been arranged from melodies found afloat by the Author in Europe, during his visit in the year 1868, and others are adopted from German and English authorities. For the anonymous pages the Author assumes all responsibility.

It is confidently hoped that this work, prepared in the love of souls, and in the faith of the Gospel of Jesus Christ, will supply a want in the means of worship, which shall secure for it the name which has been adopted: "New Standard Singer."

New York, March 1st, 1869.

Philip Phillips

Smith & McDougal, Stereotypers and Electrotypers, 82 & 84 Beekman St., New York.

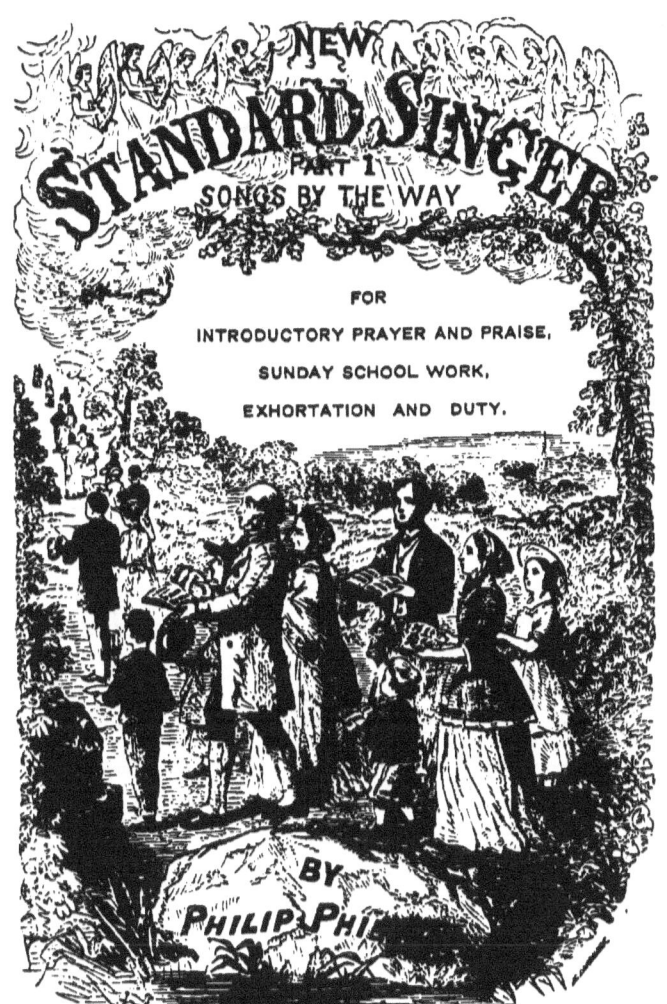

NEW

STANDARD SINGER
PART 1
SONGS BY THE WAY

FOR

INTRODUCTORY PRAYER AND PRAISE,

SUNDAY SCHOOL WORK,

EXHORTATION AND DUTY.

BY

PHILIP PHI

PHILIP PHILLIPS, Author and Publisher,
805 BROADWAY, NEW YORK.

HITCHCOCK & WALDEN,
CINCINNATI, CHICAGO, AND ST. LOUIS.

No. 1

He leads us on.

PHILIP PHILLIPS.

" He leadeth me in the paths of righteousness for his Name's sake.

He leads us on by paths we did not know, Up-wards he leads us

though our steps are slow. Though oft we faint and falter by the way, Tho' storms and darkness

oft ob-scure the day. But when the clouds are gone, We know he leads us on, He

leads us on, He leads us on. He leads us on, He leads us on, He leads us on.

2	3
He leads us on through all the trying years, Past all our dreamland hopes and doubts and fears, He guides our steps through all the tangled maze, In paths of peace and wisdom's pleasant ways. *Refrain—But when, &c*	And he at last, after the weary strife, Will lead us home to everlasting life. No parting there, or pain on that bright shore, We'll meet dear friends and sing for evermore, *Refrain—But when, &c*

"The Old, Old Story."

No. 2.   T. C. O'KANE.

" The love of Christ which passeth knowledge."

1. Tell me the old, old sto - ry Of unseen things above, Of Je-sus and his
glo - ry, Of Je - sus and his love. Tell me the sto- ry sim - ply, As
to a lit- tle child, Tell me the old, old sto - ry, It will my spir-it
move; Oh, tell me the old, old sto - ry Of Je-sus and his love.

D. S. For I am weak and
wea - ry, And help-less and de -filed.

CHORUS.

2 Tell me the story slowly,
    That I may take it in,
That wonderful redemption,
    God's remedy for sin.
Tell me the story often,
    For I forget so soon!
The "early dew" of morning
    Has passed away at noon.

3 Tell me the same old story,
    When you have cause to fear
That this world's empty glory
    Is costing me too dear.
Oh, yes, when that world's glory
    Is dawning on my soul,
Tell me the old, old story,
    "Christ Jesus makes thee whole!"

Jesus, blessed Jesus.

No. 3   S. J. VAIL.

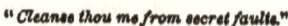

"Cleanse thou me from secret faults."

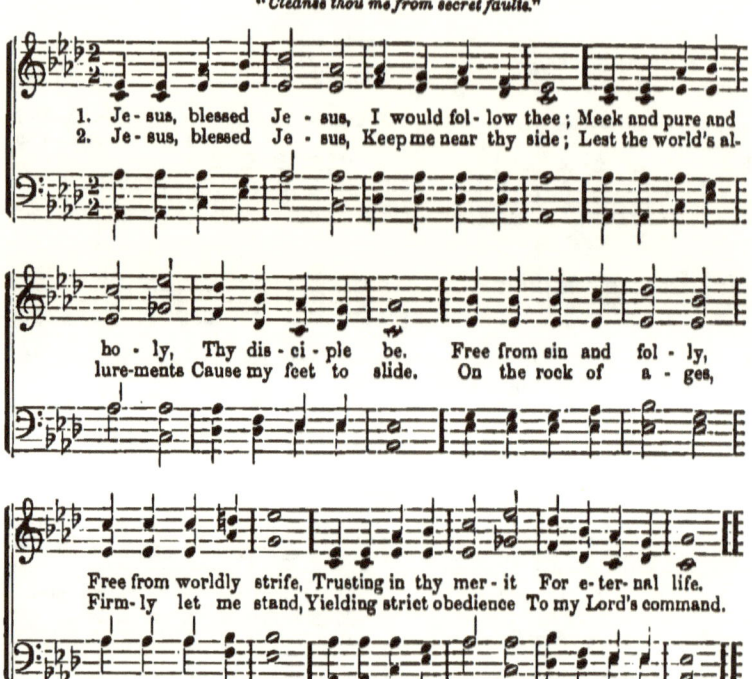

1. Je - sus, blessed Je - sus, I would fol - low thee; Meek and pure and
2. Je - sus, blessed Je - sus, Keep me near thy side; Lest the world's al-

ho - ly, Thy dis - ci - ple be. Free from sin and fol - ly,
lure-ments Cause my feet to slide. On the rock of a - ges,

Free from worldly strife, Trusting in thy mer - it For e - ter - nal life.
Firm-ly let me stand, Yielding strict obedience To my Lord's command.

3 Purer yet and purer
  I would be in mind,
Dearer yet and dearer
  Every duty find;
Hoping still and trusting
  God without a fear,
Patiently believing
  He will make all clear.

4 Calmer yet and calmer
  Trial bear and pain,
Surer yet and surer
  Peace at last to gain;
Suffering still and doing,
  To his will resigned,
And to God subduing
  Heart, and will, and mind.

5 Higher yet and higher
  Out of clouds and night,
Nearer yet and nearer
  Rising to the light—
Light serene and holy,
  Where my soul may rest,
Purified and lowly,
  Sanctified and blest.

6 Quicker yet and quicker
  Ever onward press,
Firmer yet and firmer
  Step as I progress:
Oft these earnest longings
  Swell within my breast;
Yet their inner meaning
  Ne'er can be expressed.

Saviour and Friend.

" The Lord is my light."

1. Rest of the wea - ry, Joy of the sad,
2. Pil - low where ly - ing, Love rests its head,

Hope of the drea - ry, Light of the glad;
Peace of the dy - ing, Life of the dead;

Home of the stran - ger, Strength to the end,
Path of the low - ly, Prize at the end,

Re - fuge from dan - ger, Sa - viour and Friend.
Breath of the ho - ly, Sa - viour and Friend.

3 When my feet stumble,
  I'll to Thee cry ;
Crown of the humble,
  Cross of the high.
When my steps wander,
  Over me bend,
Truer and fonder,
  Saviour and Friend.

4 Ever confessing
  Thee, I will raise
Unto thee blessing,
  Glory and praise;
All my endeavour,
  World without end,
Thine to be ever,
  Saviour and Friend.

Seek the Saviour.

No. 5.   GEO. F. ROOT.

"O God, thou art my God, early will I seek thee."

1. Seek the Sa - viour! tho' a - round thee, Drops a dark and dis - mal

cloud, Though it feels so deep and hea - vy on a heart with sor-row

bowed, Seek him quick-ly, time is pass-ing, Pass-ing ra - pid-ly a -

way, Lis-ten to the words that tell you, There is still a brighter day.

2

Seek the Saviour! though life's tempest
   May unfurl life's chilling blast;
There is hope for thee my brother,
   Storms will not for ever last.
Don't give up, and cry forsaken!
   Don't begin to say you're lost:
Look! there comes a gleam of sunshine;
   See what your redemption cost.

3

Seek the Saviour! don't be grieving
   O'er that darksome billow there;
Life's a sea of stormy billows,
   We must meet them everywhere;
Pass right through them, do not tarry,
   Overcome the heaving tide,
There's a sparkling gleam of sunshine
   Waiting on the other side.

No. 6   # Eternal Life.   PHILIP PHILLIPS.

"Fight the good fight of faith; lay hold on eternal life."

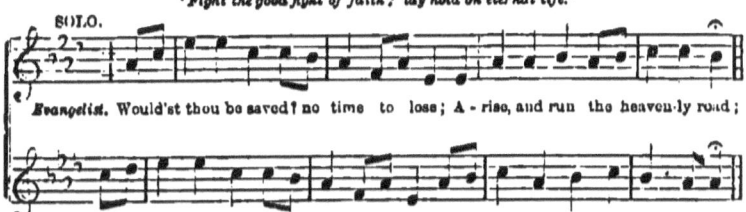

Evangelist. Would'st thou be saved? no time to lose; A - rise, and run the heaven-ly road;

Would'st thou be blest? then, pil - grim, haste To leave des-truc tion's dread abode.

CHORUS.

O come! (O come!) the Sa - viour calls, "I am the way, the
echo.

truth, the life;" Come hith - er, burdened soul, to me.

Pilgrim.	*Pilgrim.*

O, tell me how! O, tell me where!
 The way I long have sought to know;
 But fear the guilt and sin I bear
 Will sink me in the depths of woe.
     O, come, etc.
	God's word shall guide me; yes, I see
	 A light from yonder distant hill;
	 O, tell me, does it shine for me?
	 Hail, glorious light! I will, I will!
	     O, come, etc.

Evangelist.	*Pilgrim.*

God's word will guide thee; dost thou see
 A light from yonder distant hill?
 On, Pilgrim, on! it shines for thee,
 With steady course pursue it still.
     O, come, etc.
	Farewell, a long farewell to those
	 Who seek to stay me as I fly;
	 My ears against their call I close,
	 Life, life, eternal life! my cry.
	     O, come, etc.

NOTE.—This song may be sung as a Duet between the Teachers and the School; or when rendered as Solos (in dialogue), the Chorus should be sung from another room or gallery out of sight, as an echo.

No 7   **Our Sabbath Home.**   W. HALEY.

" O how amiable are thy dwellings, thou Lord of Hosts."

1. O - pen now thy gates of beau - ty! Zi - on, let me

en - ter there, Where my soul, in joy - ful du - ty,

Waits for him that an - swers pray'r. Oh how bless - ed

is this place, Filled with so - lace, light, and grace.

2 Here thy praise is gladly chanted,
    Here thy seed is duly sown ;
Let my soul, where it is planted,
    Bring forth precious sheaves alone :
So that all I hear may be
Fruitful unto life in me.

3 Yes, my God, I come before thee,
    Come thou also down to me ;
Where we find thee and adore thee,
    There a heaven on earth must be :
To my heart, oh, enter thou,
Let it be thy temple now.

Nature's Song. C. M. Double.

No. 8   GIARDINI.

" God said, Let the earth bring forth grass.."

1. There's not a tint that paints the rose, Or decks the lil - y fair,

Or streaks the humblest flower that blows, But God has placed it there.

At ear - ly dawn there's not a gale, A- cross the landscape driven,

And not a breeze that sweeps the vale, That is not sent by heaven.

2.

There's not of grass a single blade,
    Or leaf of loveliest green,
Where heavenly skill is not displayed,
    And heavenly wisdom seen.
Around, beneath, below, above,
    Wherever space extends,
There God displays his boundless love,
    And power with mercy blends.

No. 9.   # The Water of Life.*   WM. B. BRADBURY.

"I will give unto him that is athirst of the fountain of the water of life freely."

1. { Je - sus the wa-ter of life will give Free - ly, free - ly, free - ly;
Come to that fountain, O drink and live, Free - ly, free - ly, free - ly;

Jesus the water of life will give Freely to those who love him.
Come to that fountain, O drink and live, Flowing for those that . . love him.

Spirit and the Bride say come, Free-ly, free-ly, free-ly, And he that is thirsty, let him come And

drink of the water of life . . The fountain of life is flow-ing, Flow-ing, free-ly

flow - ing, The fountain of life is flow - ing, Is flowing for you and for me. . .

* From "FRESH LAURELS," by permission of Biglow & Main.

2 Jesus has promised a home in heaven,
  Freely, freely, freely ;
  Jesus has promised a home in heaven,
  Freely to those that love him.
  Treasures unfading will there be given,
  Freely, freely, freely ;
  Treasures unfading will there be given,
  Freely to those that love him. *Cho.*

3 Jesus has promised a robe of white,
  Freely, freely, freely ;
  Jesus has promised a robe of white,
  Freely to those that love him ;

Kingdoms of glory and crowns of light,
  Freely, freely, freely ;
  Kingdoms of glory and crown of light,
  Freely to those that love him. *Cho.*

4 Jesus has promised eternal day,
  Freely, freely, freely ;
  Jesus has promised eternal day,
  Freely to those that love him :
  Pleasure that never shall pass away,
  Freely, freely, freely ;
  Pleasure that never shall pass away,
  Freely to those that love him. *Cho.*

No. 10   'Tis Blessed to Give.   PHILIP PHILLIPS.

" God loveth the cheerful giver."

1. { As God has kindly blessed us, To others let us give ; }
   { Not with a grudging spirit, Or that our deeds may live : } Not with a vain am-
D.C.   No merit in a kindness That claims reward again. *(Go on to Chorus.)*

bi - tion, To win the praise of men.   Now in the name of Je - sus, Our

alms we should bestow ; God loves a cheerful giv-er : the Bi-ble tells us so.

2 Now in the world before us
    A glorious field we see ;
  And in our Master's vineyard
    How active we should be.
  The Sabbath schools around us,
    For help they loudly call ;
  Home missions, too, remember,
    And freely give to all. *Cho.*

3 The cause of foreign missions
    Our zealous care demands ;
  We'll send the blessed Bible
    To distant heathen lands,
  · That they may hear of Jesus,
    Whom we so dearly love ;
  May leave their senseless idols,
    And worship God above. *Cho.*

All Things Earnest.

No. 11   JOSEPH DYER.

"My days are swifter than a weaver's shuttle."

Very slowly and pathetically.

Time is earnest, Passing by; Death is earnest, Drawing nigh;

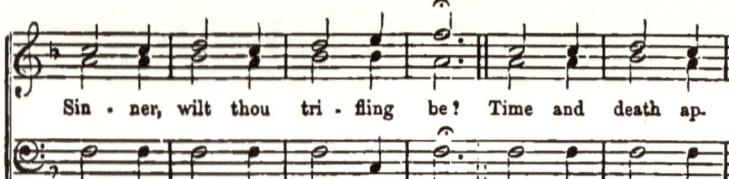

Sin - ner, wilt thou tri - fling be? Time and death ap-

peal to thee, Time and death ap - peal to thee.

2.

Life is earnest:
When 'tis o'er,
Thou returnest
Never more;
Soon to meet Eternity,
Wilt thou never serious be?

3.

Heaven is earnest:
Solemnly
Float its voices
Down to thee.
O thou mortal, art thou gay,
Sporting through thine earthly day?

4.

Hell is earnest:
Fiercely roll
Burning billows
Near thy soul.
Woe for thee, if thou abide
Unredeemed, unsanctified!

5.

God is earnest:
Kneel and pray
Ere thy season
Pass away;
Ere be set his judgment throne,
Vengeance ready, mercy gone.

6.

Christ is earnest:
Bids thee, "Come!"
Paid thy spirit's
Priceless sum.
Wilt thou spurn thy Saviour's love,
Pleading with thee from above?

No. 12 ## In Wrath remember Mercy.

" Hold thou me up and I shall be safe."

1. Gent-ly, gent-ly lay thy rod On my sin-ful head, O God;
2. Heal me, for my flesh is weak; Heal, me for thy grace I seek;

Stay thy wrath, in mer-cy stay, Lest I sink be-fore its sway.
This my on-ly plea I make, Heal me for thy mer-cy's sake.

3 Who within the silent grave
Shall proclaim thy power to save?
Lord, my sinking soul reprieve,—
Speak, and I shall rise and live!

4 Lo, he comes! he heeds my plea!
Lo, he comes! the shadows flee!
Glory round me dawns once more;
Rise, my spirit, and adore!

No. 13 ## The Lord is my Shepherd.

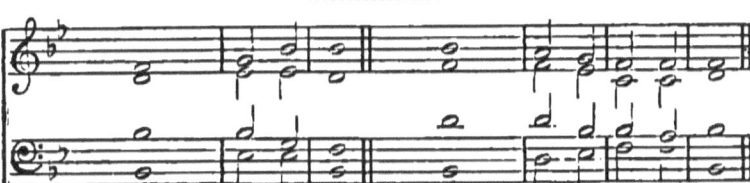

1 The Lord is my Shepherd, I | shall not | want:
He maketh me to lie down in green pastures; he leadeth me be- | side the | still— | waters.

2 He restoreth my soul; he leadeth me in the paths of righteousness, for his | name's— | sake.
Yea, though I walk through the valley of the shadow of death, I will fear no evil; for thou art with me, thy rod and thy | staff, they | comfort | me.

3 Thou preparest a table before me in the presence of mine enemies; thou anointest my head with oil, my | cup runneth | over.
Surely goodness and mercy shall follow me all the days of my life, and I shall dwell in the | house of-the | Lord for | ever.　　　　PSALM xxiii.

Pilgrims of the Night.

No. 14   Arr. by J. Bowling.

" Are they not all ministering spirits, sent forth to minister for them who shall be heirs of heaven ? "

1. Hark! hark! my soul,   an - gel - ic songs are swelling, O'er earth's green fields, and ocean's wave-beat shore; How sweet the truth those blessed strains are telling, Of that new life, where sin shall be no more.

CHORUS. *Allegretto.*

An - gels of Je - sus! An-gels of light, Sing-ing to welcome the pilgrims of the night, Singing to welcome the pilgrims of the night.

2.

Darker than night, life's shadows close
  around us,   [mark ;
And like benighted men we miss our
God hides himself, and grace has scarcely
  found us,   [dark.
Ere death finds out his victims in the
    Angels of Jesus, &c.

3.

Onward we go, for still we hear them
  singing   [come."
"Come, weary souls, for Jesus bids you
And through the dark, it echoes gently
  ringing,
The music of the Gospel leads us home.
    Angels of Jesus, &c.

4.

Cheer up my soul ! Faith's moonbeams
  softly glisten   [sea ;
Upon the breast of life's most troubled
And it will cheer thy drooping heart to
  listen   [mean for thee.
To those brave songs which angels
    Angels of Jesus, etc.

5.

Angels, sing on, your faithful watches
  keeping,   [above,
Sing us sweet fragments of the songs
While we toil on, and soothe ourselves
  with weeping,   [less love,
Till life's long night shall break in end-
    Angels of Jesus, etc.

No. 15   # The Pilgrim Invited.

"Turn, turn ye, for why will ye die !"

1. { Pil-grim, burdened with thy sin, Come the way to Zi-on's gate; }
   { There, till Mer-cy let thee in, Knock and weep, and watch and wait. }
D. C. Watch—for sa-ving grace is nigh; Wait—till heavenly light appears.

Knock—he knows the sin-ner's cry; Weep—He loves the mourner's tears;

2.

Hark ! it is the Bridegroom's voice:
Welcome, pilgrim, to thy rest ;
Now within the gate rejoice,
Safe and sealed, and bought and blest.
Safe—from all the lures of vice,
Sealed—by signs the chosen know,
Bought—by love and life the price,
Blest—the mighty debt to owe.

3.

Holy pilgrim ! what for thee
In a world like this remain?
From thy guarded breast shall flee
Fear and shame, and doubt and pain
Fear—the hope of heaven shall fly,
Shame—from glory's view retire,
Doubt—in certain rapture die,
Pain—in endless bliss expire.

2

A Song in the Night.

No. 16

"He will give His angels charge over thee."

1. My Sa-viour, be thou near me, Through life's night; I
cry, and thou wilt hear me, Be my Light! My dim sight ach-ing,
Gent-ly thou'rt making Meet for a-wak-ing, Where all is bright.

2 Through time's swelling ocean
     Be my guide!
From tempest's wild commotion
     Hide, O hide!

Life's crystal river
     Storms ruffle never;
Anchor me ever
     On that calm tide!

Christ our Light.

No. 17

"A Light that shineth in a dark place."

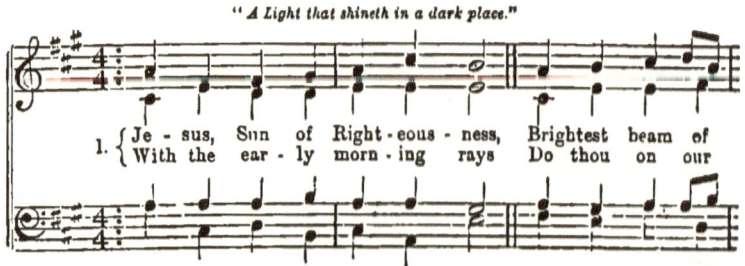

1. { Je-sus, Sun of Right-eous-ness, Brightest beam of
{ With the ear-ly morn-ing rays Do thou on our

CHRIST OUR LIGHT—*continued.*

love di - vine, darkness shine, } And dis - pel with pur - est light, All our night!

2 As on drooping herb and flower
· Falls the soft refreshing dew,
Let thy Spirit's grace and power
All our weary souls renew ;
Showers of blessing over all
Softly fall !

3 Like the sun's reviving ray,
May thy love with tender glow
All our coldness melt away,
Warm and cheer us forth to go ;
Gladly serve thee and obey
All the day !

4 Oh, our only hope and guide !
Never leave us nor forsake:
Keep us ever at thy side,
Till th' eternal morning break ;
Moving on to Zion hill
Homeward still !

5 Lead us all our days and years
In thy straight and narrow way ;
Lead us through the vale of tears
To the land of perfect day,
Where thy people, fully blest,
Safely rest !

No. 18

God is Near Thee.

" Thou art near, O Lord."

1. God is near thee, therefore cheer thee, Sad soul ! He'll de -

fend thee, when around thee Billows roll, When around thee billows roll.

2 Calm thy sadness, look in gladness,
On high !
Faint and weary, pilgrim, cheer thee,
Help is nigh !
Pilgrim, cheer thee, help is nigh !

3 Mark the sea-bird wildly wheeling
Through the skies !

God defends him, God attends him,
When he cries !
God attends him when he cries.

4 God is near thee, therefore cheer thee,
Sad soul !
He'll defend thee, when around thee
Billows roll,
When around thee billows roll.

Sweet Spirit, Comfort Me.

No. 19   ENGLISH.

"He shall give His angels charge over thee."

1. In the time of my dis-tress, When temp-ta-tions me op-
2. When I lie within my bed, Sick in heart, and sick in

press, And when I my sins con-fess, Sweet Spi-rit, comfort me.
head, And with doubts discom-fit-ed, Sweet Spi-rit, comfort me.

3.
When the house doth sigh and weep,
And the world is drown'd in sleep,
Yet mine eyes the watch do keep,
　　Sweet Spirit, comfort me.

4.
When the judgment is reveal'd,
And that opened which was sealed,
When to Thee I have appealed,
　　Sweet Spirit, comfort me.

Jesus' Love.

No. 20

"God is Love."

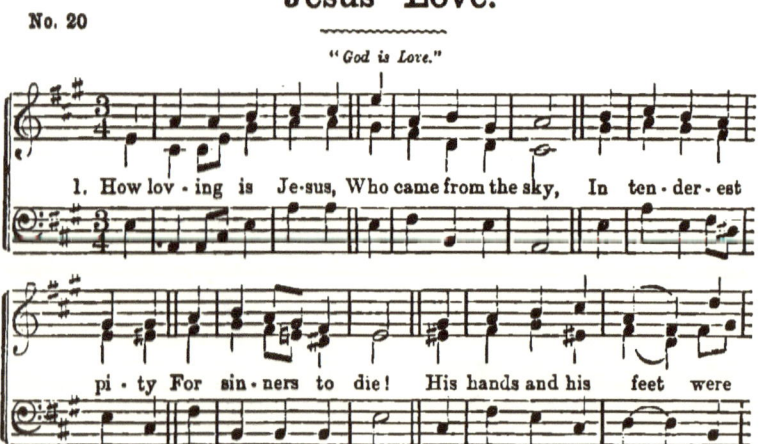

1. How lov-ing is Je-sus, Who came from the sky, In ten-der-est

pi-ty For sin-ners to die! His hands and his feet were

JESUS' LOVE—*continued.*

nail'd to the tree, And all this he suffer'd for you and for me.

2 How gladly does Jesus
Free pardon impart,
To all who receive him
By faith in their heart!
No evil befals them; their home is above,
And Jesus throws round them the arms
of his love.

3 How precious is Jesus
To all who believe ;
And out of his fulness
What grace they receive !

When weak he supports them ; when
erring he guides,
And everything needful he kindly pro-
vides.

4 O give, then, to Jesus
Your earliest days :
They only are blessèd
Who walk in his ways ;
In life and in death he will still be your
Friend,   [end.
For whom Jesus loves, he loves to the

No. 21

How Much I Owe.

" I have loved thee."

FINE.

1. When this pass-ing world is done, When has sunk yon glar - ing suu,
D. C.—Then, Lord, shall I ful - ly know—Not till then—how much I owe.

When I stand with Christ in glory, Looking o'er life's finish'd sto-ry ;—D. C.

2 When I stand before the throne,
Dressed in beauty not my own ;
When I see thee as thou art,—
Love thee with unsinning heart ;
Then, Lord, shall I fully know—
Not till then—how much I owe.

3 E'en on earth, as through a glass,
Darkly let thy glory pass ;
Make forgiveness feel so sweet.

Make thy Spirit's help so meet ;
E'en on earth, Lord, make me know
Something of how much I owe.

4 Chosen not for good in me,
Wakened up from wrath to flee ;
Hidden in the Saviour's side,
By the Spirit sanctified :
Teach me, Lord, on earth to show
By my love, how much I owe.

No. 22   # The Glorious Ship.   T. C. O'KANE.

" Except these abide in the ship, ye cannot be saved."

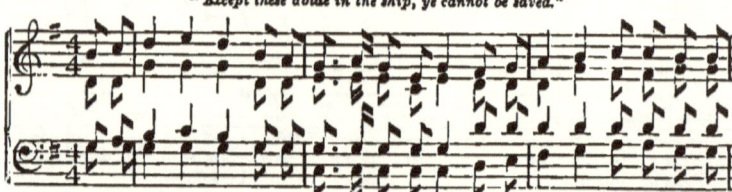

1. We are on the deep, we are sailing to our home, In the land beyond the shores of

time, Where the wea - ry rest, and no sor-rows e-ver come, In that
D.S. *" We will stand the storm," we will safe at an-chor ride, In the*

FINE.   CHORUS.

brighter, bet-ter, hap-pier clime. In the old ship Zi - on we are
port on Canaan's peace-ful shore.

sai - ing on the tide, Tho' the waves may dash and bil - lows roar,

2   [they swell!
We are on the deep—see our sails how full
And our standard floating proudly high,
'Tis the blood-stained banner of King
    Emmanuel ;
We will sail beneath it—"live or die."

3   [golden strand ;
We are on the deep—we are near the
Lo, the glitt'ring domes of heaven appear!

See! along the shore angels and our lov'd
    ones stand ;   [hear.
And their song of welcome, hark ! we

4   [so frail!
Are you on the deep? in the sinners bark
You will perish—leave without delay—
Come on board with us, and at once for
    glory sail,
And be saved while you are called, to-day.

Many ·Mansions.

W. Hedges.

"In my Father's house are many mansions."

1. There is a bet-ter world, they say, Oh, so bright! Oh, so bright!

Where sin and woe are done a-way, Oh, so bright! Oh, so bright!

And mu-sic fills the balm-y air, And an-gels bright and

pure are there, And harps of gold and mansions fair, Oh, so bright! Oh, so bright!

2.

No clouds e'er pass along its sky,
Happy land;
No tear-drop glistens in the eye,
Happy land!
They drink the gushing streams of grace,
And gaze upon the Saviour's face,
Whose brightness fills the holy place.
Happy land!

3.

Though we are sinners every one,
Jesus died!
And though our crown of peace is gone,
Jesus died!
We may be cleansed from every stain,
We may be crowned with bliss again,
And in that land of pleasure reign.
Jesus died!

Far, Far Away.

" There remaineth therefore a rest to the people of God."

W. HEDGES.

1. Had I the wings of a dove, I would fly, Far, far away, Far, far away,

Where not a cloud e-ver darkens the sky, Far, far a-way, Far, far a-way.

Fadeless the flow'rs in yon Eden that blow; Green, green the bow'rs where the still waters flow;

Hearts, like their garments, as pure as the snow, Far, far away, Far, far a-way.

2.

Had I the wings of a dove I would fly,
        Far, far away.
Where not a cloud ever darkens the sky,
        Far, far away.
There from all sorrow for ever I'd rest,
Leaning with love on Emmanuel's breast;
Joys never fade in the realms of the blest,
        Far, far away.

3.

Safely they dwell with the Lamb that
    was slain,   Far, far away.
Washed in his blood, in his presence
    they reign,   Far, far away.
Nothing unholy shall enter the sky ;
Nothing that maketh or loveth a lie ;
Oh, then for mercy to Christ let us fly !
        Come, come to-day.

Jesus, Best and Dearest.

" Who loved me, and gave himself for me."

1. Je - sus, name all names a - bove; Je - sus, best and dear - est;

Je - sus, fount of per - fect love, Ho-liest, tend'rest, near - - est.

Je - sus, source of grace com-plet-est; Je - sus pur - est, Je - sus sweetest,

LAST VERSE.

Je - sus, well of pow'r di - vine, Make me, keep me, seal me thine. A - men.

2   Jesus, opened me the gate
    That of old he entered,
    Who, in that most lost estate,
    Wholly on thee ventured;
    Thou, whose wounds are ever pleading,
    And thy passion interceding,
    From thy misery let me rise
    To a home in Paradise!

3   Jesus, crowned with thorns for me,
    Scourged for my transgression,
    Witnessing, through agony,
    That, thy good confession !
    Jesus, clad in purple raiment,
    For my evils making payment,
    Let not all thy woe and pain,
    Let not Calv'ry be in vain.   Amen.

No. 26   **The Beautiful Stream.**   Philip Phillips.

"And he showed me a pure river of water of life, clear as crystal, proceeding out of the throne of God and of the Lamb."

1. Oh, hast thou ne'er heard of the beautiful stream, That flows thro' our Father's

land; Its waters are bright in the heavenly light, And ripple o'er gold-en

sand: Seek now that beautiful   stream,   Seek now that beautiful

sand: Oh, seek now that beautiful   stream,

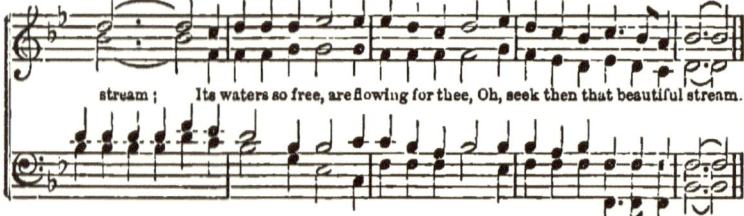

stream;   Its waters so free, are flowing for thee, Oh, seek then that beautiful stream.

Seek now that beautiful stream, so free, are flowing for thee, Oh, seek then that beautiful stream.

2
Its virtues endure, aud its waters, so pure,
Are sweet to the weary soul;
It flows from the throne of Jehovah alone,
Come, drink where its bright waves roll.
    Seek now, &c.

3
This beautiful stream is "the river of life,"
It flows for all nations free;

A balm for each wound in its waters is
Oh, sinner, it flows for thee.   [found;
    Seek now, &c.

4
Oh, wilt thou not drink of this beautiful
And dwell on its peaceful shore?   [stream,
The Spirit says, "Come all ye weary ones
And wander in sin no more."   [home,
    Seek now, &c.

No. 27

O Paradise!

B. J. WHALL.

"In my Father's house are many mansions."

With spirit.

1. O Pa - ra-dise! O Pa - ra-dise! Who does not crave for rest? Who
would not seek that hap-py land, Where those who loved are blest? Where faithful hearts and
pure, Released from sin and pain, For e - ver rest se-cure, Till Christ shall
come a - gain. O Pa-ra-dise! O Pa-ra dise! O Pa - ra - dise! A - men.

After last verse.

2
O Paradise! O Paradise!
'Tis weary waiting here,
We long to be where Jesus is,
To see and feel Him near!
Where faithful hearts and pure,
Released from sin and pain,
For ever rest secure,
Till Christ shall come again.
     O Paradise! &c.

3.
O Paradise! O Paradise!
We long to sin no more,
We long to be as pure on earth
As those on thy bright shore!

Where faithful hearts and pure,
Released from sin and pain,
For ever rest secure,
Till Christ shall come again.
     O Paradise! &c.

4.
O Father, Son, and Holy Ghost!
Most blessed One in Three!
Prepare us for that certain hope
Of never losing Thee,
Where faithful hearts and pure,
Released from sin and pain,
For ever rest secure,
Till Christ shall come again.
     O Paradise! &c.

My Heart's Desire.

No. 28

J. SCHOPPE.

" Unto you that fear my name shall the Sun of Righteousness arise."

1. Ob - ject of my first de - sire, Je - sus, cru - ci - fied for me;

All to hap - pi - ness a - spire; I would seek it, Lord, in thee:

Thee to praise, and thee to know, Makes the joy of saints be - low:

Thee to see, and thee to love, Makes the bliss of saints a - bove.

2   Lord, it is not life to live,
    If thy presence thou deny :
    Lord, if thou thy presence give,
    'Tis no longer death to die :

Source and Giver of repose,
Only from thy love it flows :
Peace and happiness are thine ;
Mine they are, if thou art mine.

Parting Song.

No. 29

Dr. Thos. Hastings.

"I will praise thy name forever and ever."

1. Our les-son now is o'er, And we a hap-py throng, With
2. What grat-i-tude we owe, For rich-est bless-ing giv'n, Yet

grate-ful hearts u-nite once more, To raise a part-ing song.
what can lit-tle chil-dren do To serve the God of heaven.

CHORUS.

Ho-san-na, ho-san-na, Most joy-ful-ly we'll sing; Ho-

san-na, ho-san-na, To Je-sus Christ our King.

3.	4.
He never will despise	We'll praise him for his word,
The smallest of our race;	We'll praise him for his love,
And he'll regard the humble cries	We'll praise him that our souls have heard,
Of all who seek his face.	His message from a bove.
Cho.—Hosanna, &c.	*Cho.*—Hosanna, &c.

Sabbath Hours. 6's.

W. HOLLIS.

" Verily, my sabbaths shall ye keep."

1. The light of Sab-bath eve Is fad-ing fast a-way;
What re-cord will it leave, To crown the clos-ing day?
Is it a Sab-bath spent, Of fruit-less time des-troyed?
Or have these mo-ments lent, Been sa-cred-ly em-ployed?

2.

How dreadful and how drear,
In yon dark world of pain,
Will Sabbaths lost appear,
That cannot come again!
Then, in that hopeless place,
The wretched souls will say,
"I had those hours of grace,
But cast them all away."

3.

To waste these Sabbath hours,
O may we never dare;
Or taint with thoughts of ours
These sacred days of prayer;
But may our Sabbaths here
Inspire our hearts with love,
And prove a foretaste clear
Of that sweet rest above.

This I Did for Thee.*

No. 31.

"What hast thou done for me."

Arranged by W. Schultz.

Adagio tristamente.

pp

1. I.... gave my life for thee, My precious blood I shed,

cresc.

That thou might'st ran-somed be, And quickened from the dead.

accel.

f I gave my life for thee, for thee, I gave my life for thee,

agitato.

ff What hast thou given for me, for me? What hast thou given for me?

2 I spent long years for thee
  In weariness and woe,
  That one eternity
  Of joy thou mightest know;
|: I spent long years for thee; :|
  Hast thou spent one for me?

3 My Father's house of light,
  My rainbow-circled throne,
  I left for earthly night,
  For wand'rings sad and lone;
|: I left it all for thee; :|
  Hast thou left aught for me?

4 I suffered much for thee,—
  More than thy tongue can tell,
  Of bitterest agony,
  To rescue thee from hell;
|: I suffered much for thee; :|
  What dust thou bear for me?

5 And I have brought to thee,
  Down from my house above,
  Salvation full and free,
  My pardon and my love;
|: Great gifts I brought to thee; :|
  What hast thou brought to me?

6 Oh, let thy life be given,
  Thy years for me be spent,
  World fetters all be riven,
  And joy with suffering blent
|: Give thou thyself to me, :|
  And I will welcome thee!

* Motto placed under a print of Christ on the Cross, in the study of a German clergyman. It is said that Count Zinzendorf was first taught to love the Saviour by reading this motto.

No. 32   **Mear.** C.M.   A. WILLIAMS.

" The day of the Lord will come as a thief in the night."

1. That aw - ful day will sure - ly come, Th'appointed hour makes haste,
2. Je - sus, thou source of all my joys, Thou ru - ler of my heart,

When I must stand be - fore my Judge, And pass the so - lemn test.
How could I bear to hear thy voice Pronounce the word,—De - part?

3 What, to be banished from my Lord,
     And yet forbid to die ;
To linger in eternal pain,
     And death for ever fly ?

4 O wretched state of deep despair,
     To see my God remove,
And fix my doleful station where
     I must not taste his love.

No. 33

GOD moves in a mysterious way,
     His wonders to perform ; -
He plants his footsteps iu the sea,
     And rides upon the storm.

2 His purposes will ripen fast,
     Unfolding every hour :
The bud may have a bitter taste,
     But sweet will be the flower.

3 Blind unbelief is sure to err,
     And scan his work in vain :
God is his own interpreter,
     And he will make it plain.

No. 34

HOW blest the children of the Lord,
     Who, walking in his sight,
Make all the precepts of his word
     Their study and delight !

2 That precious wealth shall be their
     Which cannot know decay; [dower
Which moth or rust shall ne'er devour.
     Nor spoiler take away.

3 For them that heavenly light shall
     Whose cheering rays illume [spread,
The darkest hours of life, and shed
     A halo round the tomb.

Hear my Voice. C. M.

No. 35

JOHANN CRÜGER.

"I am the Good Shepherd."

1. There is a lit - tle love - ly fold, Whose flock the Shep-herd keeps,
2. By e - vil beast, or burn-ing sky, Or damp of mid-night air,

Through sum-mer's heat and win-ter's cold, With eye that ne - ver sleeps.
Not one in all that flock shall die, Be - neath that Shepherd's care.

3.

For if, unheeding or beguiled,
In danger's path they roam,
His pity follows through the wild,
And guards them safely home.

4.

O gentle Shepherd, still behold
Thy helpless charge in me,
And take a wanderer to thy fold,
That humbly turns to thee.

No. 36

1.

THERE is a path that leads to God,
All others lead astray ;
Narrow, but pleasant, is the road,
And Christians love the way.

2.

It leads straight through this world of sin,
And dangers must be passed ;
But those who boldly walk therein,
Will come to heaven at last.

3.

But, lest my feeble steps should slide,
Or wander from thy way ;
Lord, condescend to be my guide,
And I shall never stray.

4.

Thus I may safely venture through,
Beneath my Shepherd's care ;
And keep the gate of heaven in view,
Till I shall enter there.

No. 37

1.

THERE is a glorious world above,
Where sorrow is unknown,
A city bright, a land of love,
Formed for the good alone.

2.

There gates of pearl and streets of gold,
Will strike our wond'ring sight ;
And music sweet, and bliss untold,
Will fill us with delight. '

3.

There happy spirits sigh no more ;
Their tears are wiped away ;
The Saviour's name they now adore,
Through one eternal day.

4.

There pilgrims meet from every land,
Their toils and troubles o'er ;
And friends, in one delightful band,
Are joined, to part no more.

No. 38

Uxbridge. L.M.

LOWELL MASON.

" Because thou hast been my help ; therefore in the shadow of thy wings will I rejoice."

1. God is the re-fuge of his saints, When storms of sharp distress in-vade ;
2. Loud may the troubled o - cean roar ; In sa-cred peace our souls a - bide,

Ere we can of - fer our com-plaints, Be-hold him present with his aid.
While ev-ery na-tion, ev - ery shore, Trembles, and dreads the swelling tide.

No. 39

1.

WHILE life prolongs its precious light,
   Mercy is found, and peace is given ;
But soon, ah, soon, approaching night
   Shall blot out every hope of heaven.

2.

Soon, borne on time's most rapid wing,
   Shall death command you to the grave ;
Before his bar your spirits bring,
   And none be found to hear or save.

3.

Now, God invites ; how blest the day !
   How sweet the gospel's charming sound !
Come, sinners, haste, O haste away,
   While yet a pard'ning God is found.

No. 40

1.

HOW precious is the book divine,
   By inspiration given ;
Bright as a lamp its doctrines shine,
   To guide our souls to heaven.

2.

It sweetly cheers our drooping hearts
   In this dark vale of tears ;
And life and light, and joy imparts,
   And banishes our fears.

3.

This lamp, through all the tedious night
   Of life, shall guide our way ;
Till we behold the clearer light
   Of an eternal day.

Our Glorious King. C.M. double.

No. 41

GIORNIVICHI.

"Who is like Thee, glorious in holiness, fearful in praises, doing wonders?"

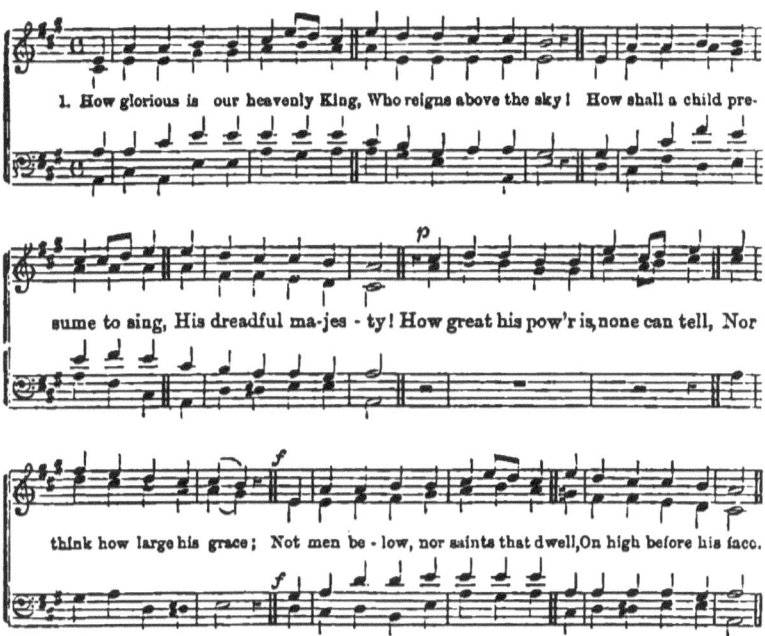

1. How glorious is our heavenly King, Who reigns above the sky! How shall a child pre-

sume to sing, His dreadful ma-jes - ty! How great his pow'r is, none can tell, Nor

think how large his grace; Not men be - low, nor saints that dwell, On high before his face.

2 Not angels, that stand round the Lord,
  Can search his secret will ;
  But they perform his heavenly word,
  And sing his praises still.

Then let me join this holy train,
  And my first offerings bring;
  The eternal God will not disdain
  To hear an infant sing.

No 42

1.

THE Bible tells us "God is Light,"
  A light we cannot see ;
Too dazzling far for our weak sight,
  So wonderful is he!
The Bible tells us "God is Love ;"
  Not all that dwell below,
Nor all that dwell in heaven above,
  Such love and pity show

2.

And though we cannot see his face,
  While we on earth remain :
The Lord will always grant us grace,
  And make our pathway plain.
Led by his light, our feet shall move
  With joy in wisdom's ways ;
Led by his love, our love we prove,
  By living to his praise.

No. 43   **Pleyel.** 5th P.M.   J. PLEYEL.

" Repent ye, for the kingdom of heaven is at hand."

> 1. Hasten, sin - ner, to   be wise, Stay not for   the   morrow's sun;
> 2. Hasten, mer - cy, to   im-plore, Stay not for   the   morrow's sun;

> Wisdom if   you still de - spise, Harder is   it   to   be won.
> Lest thy sea - son should be o'er Ere this eve - ning's stage be   run.

3 Hasten, sinner, to return,
  Stay not for the morrow's sun ;
  Lest thy lamp should fail to burn
  Ere salvation's work is done.

4 Hasten, sinner, to be blest,
  Stay not for the morrow's sun,
  Lest perdition thee arrest
  . Ere the morrow is begun.

No. 44

CHILDREN of the heavenly King,
  As we journey let us sing ;
Sing our Saviour's worthy praise,
Glorious in his works and ways.

2 We are trav'ling home to God,
  In the way our fathers trod ;
  They are happy now, and we
  Soon their happiness shall see.

3 Fear not, brethren, joyful stand
  On the borders of our land ;
  Jesus Christ, our Father's Son,
  Bids us undismay'd go on.

4 Lord ! obediently we'll go,
  Gladly leaving all below :
  Only thou our leader be,
  And we still will follow thee.

No. 45

COME, my soul, thy suit prepare ;
  Jesus loves to answer prayer ;
He himself invites thee near,
Bids thee ask him, waits to hear.

2 Lord, I come to thee for rest ;
  Take possession of my breast ;
  There thy blood-bought right maintain
  And without a rival reign.

3 While I am a pilgrim here,
  Let thy love my spirit cheer ;
  As my guide, my guard, my friend,
  Lead me to my journey's end.

4 Show me what I have to do ;
  Every hour my strength renew ;
  Let me live a life of faith,
  Let me die thy people's death.

Horton. 4 lines 7's.

No. 46   Von Wartensee.

"He ever liveth to make intercession for us."

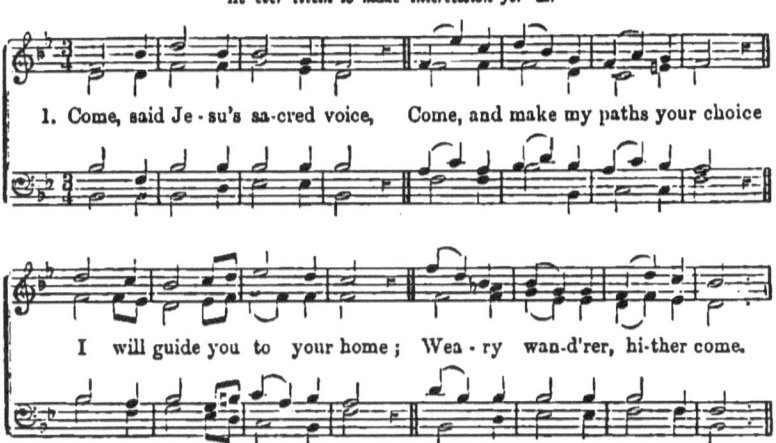

1. Come, said Je-su's sa-cred voice, Come, and make my paths your choice

I will guide you to your home; Wea-ry wan-d'rer, hi-ther come.

2.
Thou who, homeless and forlorn,
Long hast borne the proud world's scorn,
Long hast roamed the barren waste,
Weary wanderer, hither haste.

3.
Ye who, tossed on beds of pain,
Seek for ease, but seek in vain;

Ye, by fiercer anguish torn,
In remorse for guilt who mourn :—

4.
Hither come ! for here is found
Balm that flows for every wound ;
Peace that ever shall endure,
Rest eternal, sacred, sure.

No. 47

1.

WHEN thy mortal life is fled, [spread,
When the death-shades o'er thee
When is finished thy career,
Sinner, where wilt thou appear ?

2.
When the world has passed away,
When draws near the judgment-day,
When the awful trump shall sound,
Say, O where wilt thou be found ?

3.

When the Judge descends in light,
Clothed in majesty and might,
When the wicked quail with fear,
Where, O where wilt thou appear ?

4.
While the Holy Ghost is nigh,
Quickly to the Saviour fly ;
Then shall peace thy spirit cheer;
Then in heaven shalt thou appear.

Sun of my Soul.* L.M.

No. 48

'Thou art my trust from my youth.'

1. Sun of my soul, thou Sa-viour dear, It is not night if thou be near;

O may no earth-born cloud a - rise, To hide thee from thy ser-vant's eyes.

2.

Abide with me from morn till eve,
For without thee I cannot live ;
Abide with me when night is nigh,
For without thee I dare not die.

3.

If some poor wandering child of thine
Have spurned to day the voice divine
Now, Lord, the gracious work begin ;
Let him no more lie down in sin.

4.

Watch by the sick ; enrich the poor
With blessings from thy boundless store ;
Be every mourner's sleep to-night,
Like infant's slumbers, pure and light.

5.

Come near and bless us when we wake,
Ere through the world our way we take,
Till in the ocean of thy love
We lose ourselves in heaven above.

No. 49　　Tune " Lenox." P. 91.

ARISE, my soul, arise ;
　Shake off thy guilty fears ;
The bleeding Sacrifice
In my behalf appears :
Before the throne my Surety stands,
My name is written on his hands.

2　Five bleeding wounds he bears,
　Received on Calvary ;
　They pour effectual prayers,
　They strongly plead for me :—
Forgive him, O forgive, they cry,
Nor let that ransom'd sinner die.

3　The Father hears him pray,
　His dear anointed One :
　He cannot turn away
　The presence of his Son :
His Spirit answers to the blood,
And tells me I am born of God.

No. 50　　Tune, " Lenox."

YOUNG men and maidens, raise
　Your tuneful voices high ;
Old men and children, praise
The Lord of earth and sky :
The year of jubilee is come ;
Return, ye ransomed sinners, home.

2　The universal King
　Let all the world proclaim ;
　Let every creature sing
　His attributes and name :
The year of jubilee is come ;
Return, ye ransomed sinners, home.

3　Glory to God belongs ;
　Glory to God be given
　Above the noblest songs,
　Of all in earth and heaven :
The year of jubilee is come ;
Return, ye ransomed sinners, home.

* Sent to Mr. Phillips from Constantinople by our earnest missionary, Rev. A. G. Long.

No. 51

Arlington. c.m.

Dr. Arne.

"In the Lord put I my trust."

1. Lord, I approach the mer-cy seat, Where thou dost an - swer prayer;

There hum-bly fall be - fore thy feet, For none can pe - rish there.

2.

Thy promise is my only plea ;
With this I venture nigh:
Thou callest burdened souls to thee,
And such, O Lord, am I.

3.

O, wondrous love !—to bleed and die,
To bear the cross and shame,
That guilty sinners, such as I, ·
Might plead thy gracious name.

No. 52

1.

O FOR a heart to praise my God,
A heart from sin set free ;—
A heart that always feels thy blood,
So freely spilt for me :—

2.

A heart resign'd, submissive, meek,
My great Redeemer's throne;
Where only Christ is heard to speak,—
Where Jesus reigns alone.

3.

O for a lowly, contrite heart,
Believing. true, and clean ;
Which neither life nor death can part
From Him that dwells within :—

4.

A heart in every thought renew'd,
And full of love divine ;
Perfect, and right, and pure, and good,
A copy, Lord, of thine.

No. 53

1.

MY God, the spring of all my joys,
The life of my delights,
The glory of my brightest days,
And comfort of my nights.

2.

In darkest shades, if thou appear,
My dawning is begun ;
Thou art my soul's bright morning star.
And thou my rising sun.

3.

The opening heavens around me shine
With beams of sacred bliss,
If Jesus shows his mercy mine,
And whispers, I am his·--

4.

My soul would leave this heavy clay
At that transporting word,
Run up with joy the shining way,
To see and praise my Lord.

No. 54   **Laban.** s.m.   Dr. L. Mason.

" Now it is high time to awake out of sleep."

1. My soul be on thy guard; Ten thou-sand foes a - rise:
2. O watch, and fight, and pray; The bat - tle ne'er give o'er;

The hosts of sin are press-ing hard To draw thee from the skies.
Re - new it bold-ly ev - ery day, And help di - vine im - plore.

3.

Ne'er think the vict'ry won,
Nor lay thine armour down;
The work of faith will not be done,
Till thou obtain the crown.

4.

Then persevere till death
Shall bring thee to thy God;
He'll take thee, at thy parting breath,
To his divine abode.

No. 55

1.

COME, sound his praise abroad,
 And hymns of glory sing;
Jehovah is the sov'reign God,
 The universal King.

2.

He form'd the deeps unknown;
He gave the seas their bound;
The wat'ry worlds are all his own,
And all the solid ground.

3.

Come, worship at his throne;
Come, bow before the Lord;
We are his works, and not our own,
He form'd us by his word.

4.

To-day attend his voice,
Nor dare provoke his rod;
Come, like the people of his choice,
And own your gracious God.

No. 56

1.

COME, ye that love the Lord,
 And let your joys be known;
Join in a song with sweet accord,
 While ye surround his throne.

2.

Let those refuse to sing
Who never knew our God;
But servants of the heavenly King
May speak their joys abroad.

3.

The men of grace have found
Glory begun below:
Celestial fruit on earthly ground
From faith and hope may grow:

4.

Then let our songs abound,
And every tear be dry: [ground,
We're marching through Immanuel's
To fairer worlds on high.

No. 57   **Ortonville.** C.M.   DR. T. HASTINGS.

"And thou shalt call his name Jesus, for he shall save his people from their sins."

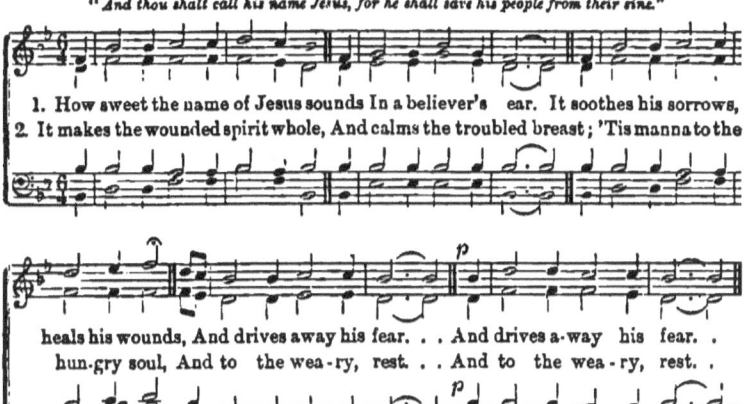

1. How sweet the name of Jesus sounds In a believer's ear. It soothes his sorrows,
2. It makes the wounded spirit whole, And calms the troubled breast; 'Tis manna to the

heals his wounds, And drives away his fear. . . And drives a-way his fear. .
hun-gry soul, And to the wea-ry, rest. . . And to the wea-ry, rest. .

3.
Dear Name, the rock on which I build,
  My shield and hiding-place ;
My never-failing treasury, fill'd
  With boundless stores of grace :

4.
Jesus, my Shepherd, Saviour, Friend,
  My Prophet, Priest, and King,
My Lord, my Life, my Way, my End,
  Accept the praise I bring.

No. 58

1.

MUST Jesus bear the cross alone,
  And all the world go free ?
No : there's a cross for every one,
  And there's a cross for me.

2.
How happy are the saints above
  Who once went sorrowing here ;
But now they taste unmingled love,
  And joy without a tear.

3.
The consecrated cross I'll bear,
  Till death shall set me free,
And then go home my crown to wear,—
  For there's a crown for me !

No. 59

1.

I LOVE to steal awhile away
  From every cumb'ring care,
And spend the hours of setting day
  In humble, grateful prayer.

2.
I love in solitude to shed
  The penitential tear,
And all his promises to plead,
  Where none but God can hear.

3.
I love to think on mercies past,
  And future good implore,—
And all my cares and sorrows cast
  On him whom I adore.

No 60 **Precious Book.** L.M.   PSALMODIST.

" His delight is in the law of the Lord."

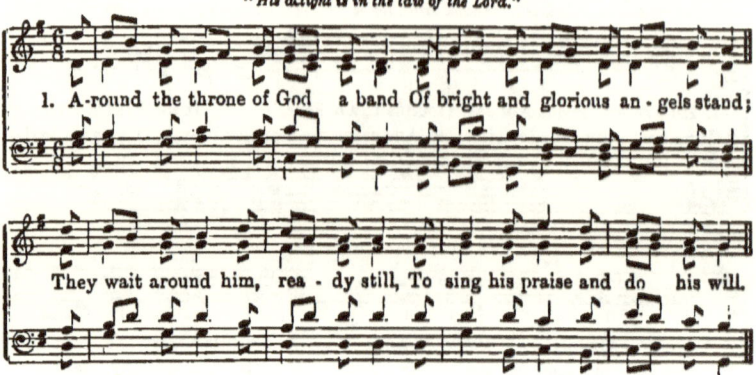

1. A-round the throne of God   a band Of bright and glorious an-gels stand;

They wait around him, rea-dy still, To sing his praise and do his will.

2.

Lord, give thine angels every day
Command to guide us on our way;
And bid them every evening keep
Their watch around us while we sleep.

3.

So shall no wicked thing draw near
To do us harm, or cause us fear;
And we shall dwell, when life is past,
With angels round thy throne at last.

No. 61

1.

LORD, thou hast searched and seen me
    through;
Thine eye commands, with piercing view,
My rising and my resting hours,
My heart and flesh, with all their powers.

2.

My thoughts, before they are my own,
Are to my God distinctly known;
He knows the words I mean to speak,
Ere from my opening lips they break.

3.

Within thy circling power I stand;
On every side 1 find thy hand:
Awake, asleep, at home, abroad,
I am surrounded still with God.

4

O may these thoughts possess my breast,
Where'er I rove, where'er I rest;
Nor let my weaker passions dare
Consent to sin, for God is there.

No. 62

1.

THIS is a precious book indeed!
    Happy the child who loves to read!
'Tis God's own word, which he has
    given,
To show our souls the way to heaven.

2.

It tells us how the world was made,
And how good men the Lord obeyed;
Here his commands are written too,
To teach us what we ought to do.

3.

It bids us all from sin to fly,
Because our souls can never die;
It points to heaven, where angels dwell,
And warns us to escape from hell.

4.

But, what is more than all beside,
The Bible tells us Jesus died;
This is its best, its chief intent,
To lead poor sinners to repent.

Nettleton. 8's & 7's, double.

No. 63

DR. NETTLETON.

"God is a spirit; and they that worship him must worship him in spirit and in truth."

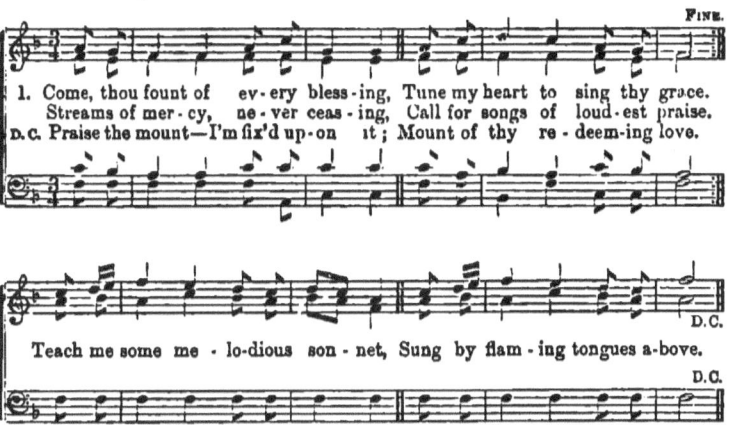

1. Come, thou fount of ev-ery bless-ing, Tune my heart to sing thy grace.
Streams of mer-cy, ne-ver ceas-ing, Call for songs of loud-est praise.
D.C. Praise the mount—I'm fix'd up-on it; Mount of thy re-deem-ing love.

Teach me some me-lo-dious son-net, Sung by flam-ing tongues a-bove.

2.

Here I'll raise mine Ebenezer ;
Hither by thy help I'm come ;
And I hope, by thy good pleasure,
Safely to arrive at home.
Jesus sought me when a stranger,
Wand'ring from the fold of God,
He, to rescue me from danger,
Interposed his precious blood.

3.

O ! to grace how great a debtor
Daily I'm constrained to be !
Let thy goodness, like a fetter,
Bind my wand'ring heart to thee :
Prone to wander, Lord, I feel it, —
Prone to leave the God I love ;
Here's my heart, O take and seal it ;
Seal it for thy courts above.

No. 64

1.

JESUS, I my cross have taken,
All to leave and follow thee ;
Naked, poor, despised, forsaken,
Thou from hence my all shalt be.
Perish every fond ambition,
All I've sought, or hoped, or known,
Yet how rich is my condition,
God and heaven are still mine own.

2.

Haste thee on from grace to glory,
Armed by faith, and winged by prayer
Heaven's eternal day before thee —
God's own hand shall guide thee there.

Soon shall close thine earthly mission,
Soon shall pass thy pilgrim days ;
Hope shall change to glad fruition,
Faith to sight, and prayer to praise.

3.

Know, my soul, thy full salvation ;
Rise o'er sin, and fear, and care ;
Joy to find in every station
Something still to do or bear ;
Think what Spirit dwells within thee :
Think what Father's smiles are thine :
Think that Jesus died to win thee :
Child of heaven, canst thou repine ?

The Heavenly Shepherd. C.M.

No. 65   REV. W. JONES.

" The Lord is my Shepherd: I shall not want."

1. The Lord him-self, the migh-ty Lord, Vouchsafes to be my Guide;

The Shep-herd, by whose con-stant care My wants are all sup-plied.

2.

In tender grass he makes me feed,
  And gently there repose ;
Then leads me to cool shades, and where
  Refreshing water flows.

3.

He does my wand'ring soul reclaim,
  And, to His endless praise,
Instruct with humble zeal to walk
  In his most righteous ways.

4.

I pass the gloomy vale of death,
  From fear and danger free ;
For there His aiding rod and staff
  Defend and comfort me.

5.

Since God does thus His wondrous love
  Through all my life extend,
That life to Him I will devote,
  And in His temple spend.

No. 66

1.

MY Shepherd is the living Lord,
  Nothing therefore I need :
In pastures fair, near pleasant streams,
  He setteth me to feed.

2.

He shall convert and glad my soul,
  And bring my mind in frame
To walk in paths of righteousness,
  For His most holy name.

3.

Yea, though I walk in vale of death,
  Yet will I fear no ill :
Thy rod and staff do comfort me,
  And Thou art with me still.

4.

Through all my life Thy favour is
  So frankly show'd to me,
That in Thy house for evermore
  My dwelling-place shall be.

No. 67 ## God Bless our School. GIARDINI.

" The knowledge of the holy is understanding."

Cheerful.

1. God bless our Sun - day School, Increase our Sun - day School,

God bless our school. Send down thy grace di - vine, May eve - ry

child be Thine, And love, all hearts entwine ; God bless our School.

2.

All our dear teachers bless,
And give them large success
  In winning souls.
May they encouraged be,
And oft around them see
Their labours crown'd by thee ;
  God bless our School.

3.

So may our school increase,
In knowledge, love, and peace ;
  God bless our school.
And when death's arrows fly,
And useful teachers die,
Their places still supply ;
  God bless our School.

No. 68

1.

THE leaves around decay,
  Their bloom has passed away,
  They now fall fast.
We, too, ere long, must die,
And in the cold earth lie,
The spring of life gone by,—
  The summer past.

2.

Yet trees will bud once more,
And leaves will clothe them o'er,
  When winter's fled ;
So we, from the deep gloom
Of the lone, silent tomb,
Shall rise, when Christ shall come
  To wake the dead.

Condescension. 7's double.

No. 69   Arr. by PHILIP PHILLIPS.

" Though He was rich, yet for our sakes He became poor."

1. Christ is mer - ci - ful and mild; He was once a lit - tle child; He, whom heavenly hosts adore, Lived on earth among the poor. Thus he laid his glory by, When for us he stooped to die: How I wonder, when I see His unbounded love to me.

2 He the sick to health restored,
To the poor he preached the word;
Even children had a share
Of his love and tender care.

Every bird can build its nest;
Foxes have their place of rest;
He who our salvation made,
Had not where to lay his head.

No. 70

1.

JESUS bids me seek his face:
 Lord, I come to ask thy grace,
Send thy Spirit from above,
Teach me to obey and love.
Unto thee I fain would go;
All I want thou canst bestow.
Precious Saviour, pity me,
To thy loving arms I flee.

2.

Wilt thou, Lord, a child receive?
Wilt thou all my sins forgive?
Oh, dissolve this heart of stone,
Make me thine, and thine alone:

Sin is present with me still;
Disobedient is my will.
Precious Saviour, pity me,
To thy loving arms I flee.

3.

Sinful thoughts too oft prevail;
Vain desires my heart assail:
Oh, my Saviour make me whole,
Form anew my inmost soul;
Kindly guard me every day,
Be my everlasting stay.
Precious Saviour, pity me,
To thy loving arms I flee.

No. 71

Holy Bible. 7's.

" O how love I thy law !"

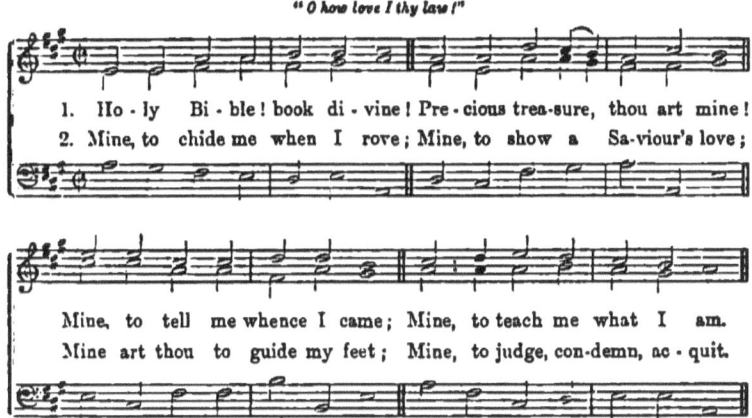

1. Ho - ly Bi - ble ! book di - vine ! Pre - cious trea-sure, thou art mine !
2. Mine, to chide me when I rove ; Mine, to show a Sa-viour's love ;

Mine, to tell me whence I came ; Mine, to teach me what I am.
Mine art thou to guide my feet ; Mine, to judge, con-demn, ac - quit.

<table>
<tr><td>

3.

Mine, to comfort in distress,
If the Holy Spirit bless ;
Mine, to show by living faith,
How to triumph over death.
</td><td>

4.

Mine, to tell of joys to come ;
Mine, to show the sinner's doom :
Holy Bible ! book divine !
Precious treasure, thou art mine !
</td></tr>
</table>

No. 72

1.

HEAR ye not a voice from heaven,
To the listening spirit given?
"Children come ! " it seems to say,
" Give your hearts to me to day."

2.

Lord, may we remember thee,
While from pain and sorrows free ;
While our day is in its dew,
And the clouds of life are few

3.

Now to thee, O Lord, we come,
In our morning's early bloom ;
Breathe on us thy grace divine,
Touch our hearts and make them thine.

No. 73

1.

CHILDREN, listen to the Lord,
And obey his gracious word ;
Seek his face with heart and mind ;
Early seek, and you shall find.

2.

Sorrowful, your sins confess ;
Plead his perfect righteousness ;
See the Saviour's bleeding side—
Come—you will not be denied.

3.

For his worship now prepare ;
Kneel to him in fervent prayer ;
Serve him with a perfect heart ;
Never from his ways depart.

Familiar Hymns.

No. 74.   *Tune, "Watcher," Key D.*

1 I want to be like Jesus,
  So lowly and so meek;
For no one marked an angry word
  That ever heard him speak.

2 I want to be like Jesus,
  So frequently in prayer;
Alone upon the mountain top,
  He met his father there.

8 I want to be like Jesus;
  I never, never find,
That he, though persecuted, was
  To any one unkind.

No. 75.   *Tune, "Horton," Key B♭.*

1 SOFTLY now the light of day
  Fades upon our sight away;
Free from care, from labor free,
Lord, we would commune with thee.

2 Soon from us the light of day
  Shall forever pass away;
Then, from sin and sorrow free,
Take us, Lord, to dwell with Thee.

No. 76.   *Tune, "Happy Day," Key G.*

1 OH, happy day that fixed my choice
On thee, my Saviour and my God!
Well may this glowing heart rejoice,
And tell its raptures all abroad.

CHORUS.

Happy day, happy day,
When Jesus washed my sins away;
He taught me how to watch and pray,
And live rejoicing every day. ~
Happy day, happy day,
When Jesus washed my sins away.

2 Oh, happy bond, that seals my vows
  To Him, who merits all my love;
Let cheerful anthems fill his house,
  While to that sacred shrine I move.
Happy day, happy day, etc.

No. 77.   *Tune, "Home of Glory," Key C.*

1 IN the Christian's home in glory,
  There remains a land of rest;
There the Saviour's gone before me,
  To fulfil my soul's request.

CHORUS.

There is rest for the weary,
There is rest for the weary,
There is rest for the weary,
  There is rest for you.
On the other side of Jordan,
In the sweet fields of Eden,
Where the tree of life is blooming,
  There is rest for you.

2 He is fitting up my mansion,
  Which eternally shall stand,
For my stay shall not be transient
  In that holy, happy land.

3 Pain nor sickness ne'er shall enter,
  Grief nor woe my lot shall share;
But in that celestial center
  I a crown of life shall wear.

4 Death itself shall then be vanquished,
  And his sting shall be withdrawn;
Shout for gladness, O ye ransomed,
Hail with joy the rising morn.

5 Sing, O sing, ye heirs of glory;
  Shout your triumph as you go;
Zion's gate will open for you,
  You shall find an entrance through.

No. 78.   *Tune, "Angel Band," Key C.*

1 My latest sun is sinking fast,
  My race is nearly run;
My strongest trials now are past,
  My triumph is begun.

REFRAIN.

O come, angel band, come and around
  me stand,
O bear me away on your snowy
  wings
  To my immortal home!
O bear me away on your snowy wings
  To my immortal home!

2 I know I'm nearing the holy ranks
  Of friends and kindred dear,
For I brush the dews on Jordan's
  banks,
  The crossing must be near.

NEW STANDARD SINGER.
PART II.

CAROLS OF PRAISE.

FOR
CHRISTMAS,
NEW YEARS',
NATIONAL,
AND THANKSGIVING DAYS.

BY PHILIP PHILLIPS.

PHILIP PHILLIPS, Author and Publisher,
805 Broadway, New York.

HITCHCOCK & WALDEN,
Cincinnati, Chicago, and St. Louis.

Happy, Happy Christmas.

No. 79   J. B. MONSELL, LL.D.

" On earth peace, good will towards men."

1. A hap-py, hap-py Christ-mas, and a mer-ry bright New Year. How sweet the kind old greet-ings sound to ev - 'ry heart and ear; No mat - ter how care - bur-den'd, and no mat - ter how de - press'd, . A some-thing in their wel-come, makes them dear to ev - 'ry breast.

2 We heard them in our childhood, when,
   With spirits light and gay,
We dreamt not that life's joyfulness
   Could ever pass away ;
And though long years of carefulness
   Have sobered many a heart,
A joy still lingers round them, which
   Can never quite depart.

3 Nor ever shall if, Christian-like,
   We count the rolling years
Not as removing joys from us,
   But sins, and cares, and tears ;

And upward, onward, bearing us
   To that bright land and blest.
Where the wicked cease from troubling,
   And the weary are at rest.

4 No matter how care-burdened, and
   No matter how depress'd,
A something in their welcome makes
   Them dear to every breast.
Long may the kind old greetings sound,
   To every heart and ear,
A happy, happy Christmas, and
   A merry, bright New Year.

The Herald Angels.

No. 80

MENDELSSOHN.

"Glory to God in the Highest."

Hark! the herald angels sing, "Glo - ry to the new-born King; Peace on earth, and mercy mild; God and sinners re - concil - ed." Joyful, all ye nations rise; Join the triumph of the skies; With th' an-gel - ic host proclaim, "Christ is born in Beth - le - hem." Hark! the he - rald an - gels sing,—Glo - ry to the new-born King.

2 Christ, by highest heaven adored,
Christ the everlasting Lord,
Late in time behold him come,
Offspring of a Virgin's womb:
Veil'd in flesh, the Godhead see,
Hail the incarnate Deity:
Pleased, as man, with men to dwell,
Jesus, our Immanuel!
Hark! the herald angels sing,
Glory to the new-born King!

3 Hail! the heaven-born Prince of Peace!
Hail! the Sun of Righteousness!
Light and life to all he brings,
Risen with healing in his wings,
Mild he lays his glory by,
Born that man no more may die:
Born to raise the sons of earth,
Born to give them second birth.
Hark! the herald angels sing,
Glory to the new-born King!

No. 81   **Christmas Carol.**   J. C. WHITE.

" For unto us is born this day in the city of David a Saviour, who is Christ the Lord."

1. { Christmas bells are ringing the blessed chime, The Saviour's born, the Saviour's born:
   { Lis-ten to the sto-ry the an-gels brought To Bethlehem's plain, to Bethlehem's plain,
2. { Hark, the ho-ly an-gels are sing-ing now, Peace on earth, good will to men:
   { Tell the wond'rous sto-ry to all the earth, From age to age, from shore to shore,

Children now are singing the joyful theme, } Christ, the Saviour, is born to-day. Carol in gladness,
In a manger ly-ing, the One long sought, }
Hasten to the manger, to Jes-us bow. } Christ, the Saviour, is born to-day. Carol ye mountains
Christmas bells shall ring out the Saviour's birth }

ca-rol in glee, Ca-rol for Je-sus, he came to save thee; Carol with hearts full of love to all,
ca-rol ye rills, Ca-rol the herds on a thousand hills; Carol ye breezes that waft our prayers,

CHORUS. *Lively.*

Ca-rol, for Je-sus has come, Ring, ring, ring, merry bells ring on, } Ring out the Old,
Ca-rol, for Je-sus is King. Ring, ring, &c. }

ring in the New, For Christ the Lord is King, let all the earth sing, Glory in the High-est.

Song of Praise.

No. 82

W. D. Gilbert.

"He is thy Lord, and worship thou him."

1. Songs of praise the au - gels sang, Heaven with hal - le - lu - jahs rang,

When Je - ho - vah's work be - gun, When he spake, and it was done.

Songs of praise a - woke the morn When the Prince of Peace was born;

Songs of praise a - rose when he Cap - tive led cap - ti - vi - ty.

2.

Heaven and earth must pass away;
Songs of praise shall crown that day:
God will make new heavens and earth;
Songs of praise shall hail their birth.
And shall man alone be dumb,
Till that glorious kingdom come?
No! the church delights to raise
Psalms, and hymns, and songs of praise.

3.

Saints below, with heart and voice,
Still in songs of praise rejoice;
Learning here, by faith and love,
Songs of praise to sing above.
Borne upon their latest breath,
Songs of praise shall conquer death;
Then, amidst eternal joy,
Songs of praise their powers employ.

No. 83   # Come and Worship.   J. McFarland.

"Good tidings of great joy to all people."

1. An-gels from the realms of glo-ry, Wing your flight o'er all the earth.

Ye who sang Cre - a - tion's sto-ry, Now pro - claim Mes-si - ah's birth.

Come and wor-ship, come and worship, Worship Christ, the new-born King.

Come and worship, come and worship, Worship Christ, the new-born King.

2 Shepherds ! in the field abiding,
   Watching o'er your flocks by night ;
   God with man is now residing,
   Yonder shines the infant-light.
   Come, etc.

3 Sages, leave your contemplations ;
   Brighter visions beam afar ;
   Seek the Great Desire of nations :
   Ye have seen his natal star.
   Come, etc.

4 Saints ! before the altar bending,
   Watching long in hope and fear,
   Suddenly the Lord, descending,
   In his temple shall appear.
   Come, etc.

5 Sinners ! wrung with true repentance,
   Doom'd for guilt to endless pains,
   Justice now revokes the sentence,
   Mercy calls you—break your chains ;
   Come, etc.

A Home in Heaven.*

No. 84.   T. C. O'KANE.

"In my Father's house are many mansions."

1. A home in heaven! what a joyful thought, As the poor man toils in his wea-ry lot,
2. A home in heaven! As the sufferer lies On his bed of pain and up-lifts his eyes

No. 85.
3. A home in heaven! When our treasures fade, And our wealth and fame in the dust are laid.
4. A home in heaven! When our friends have fled To the cheerless gloom of the mold'ring dead,

Ritard ad. lib.

His heart oppressed, and by anguish driven From his home below to his home in heaven.
To that bright home, what a joy is given, With the blessed thought of a home in heaven.
When strength decays and our health is riven, We are happy still with our home in heaven.
We rest in hope on the promise given, We shall meet up there in our home in heaven.

Chorus.

Trav'ling on   so glad and free,   To a   home   for you and me,
                  so glad and free,   for you and me,

Come and join   our pilgrim band,   Trav'ling to the promised heavenly land.
                   our pilgrim band,

* Specially contributed by the author of "FRESH LEAVES."

English Christmas Song.

No. 86

CHARLES COOTE.

" Blessed is He that cometh in the name of the Lord."

mf

1. I sing the com-ing of the Lord, Then lis-ten to my lay:

Tho' thrice six hun-dred years have fled Since that e-vent-ful day.

ff The Son of God! the Lord of Life! How won-drous are his ways!

Oh, for a harp of thousand strings, To sound a-broad his praise!

p Oh, for a harp of thousand strings! Oh, for a harp of thousand strings!

ENGLISH CHRISTMAS SONG—*continued.*

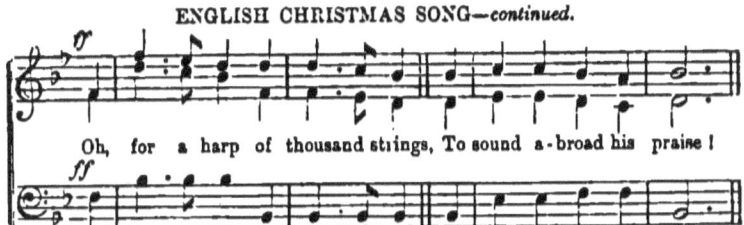

Oh, for a harp of thousand strings, To sound a-broad his praise!

2 He came not as a mighty king,
   With pomp, and power, and dread ;
Ah no ! a stable was his home,
   A manger was his bed.
But hark ! how joyful was the lay,
   How rapturous the sound,
When "Glory be to God" was sung,
   By angel hosts around !
      Oh, for a harp, &c.

3 The star was bright that led aright
   The wise men to the place,
Where love and peace were lighting up
   The Holy Infant's face.
They worshipped him, and freely gave
   Their gifts, a rich display
Of spices rare and glitt'ring gold,
   And then "went on their way."
      Oh, for a harp, &c.

4 And did he bow his sacred head,
   And die a death of shame ?—
Let men and angels magnify
   And bless his holy name.
O let us live in peace and love,
   And cast away our pride,
And crucify our sins afresh,
   As he was crucified.
      Oh, for a harp, &c.

5 He rose again,—then let us rise
   From sin, and Christ adore,
And dwell in peace with all mankind,
   And tempt the Lord no more.
The Son of God ! the Lord of Life !
   How wondrous are his ways !
Oh, for a harp of thousand strings,
   To sound abroad his praise !
      Oh, for a harp, &c.

New Year's Hymn.

No. 87

" We spend our years as a tale that is told."

1. Are there no years in heaven ? No change of day and night?

No roll-ing sea-sons' va-ried hues, To mark Time's onward flight?

2 No ; time itself must fade,
   And New Years' Days shall cease,
When all God's children meet on high,
   To hail the Prince of Peace.

3 In his great name we raise
   Our New Year Song to heaven ;
To praise our Father's boundless love,
   And ask to be forgiven.

No. 88

Antioch. C.M.

HANDEL.

"Tell ye the daughter of Sion, behold thy king cometh unto thee."

1. Joy to the world, the Lord is come! Let earth receive her King;

Let ev - 'ry heart pre - pare him room, And

heaven and na - ture sing, And heaven, and na - ture

And heaven and na - ture sing, And

sing, ... And heaven, and heaven and na - ture sing.

heaven and na - ture sing. And heaven and na - ture sing.

2 Joy to the earth, the Saviour reigns;
Let men their songs employ;
While fields and floods, rocks, hills and
plains
Repeat the sounding joy.

3 He rules the world with truth and
grace,
And makes the nations prove
The glories of his righteousness,
And wonders of his love.

A New Year's Prayer.

No. 89   Rev. R. Maguire.

" So teach us to number our days that we may apply our hearts unto wisdom.

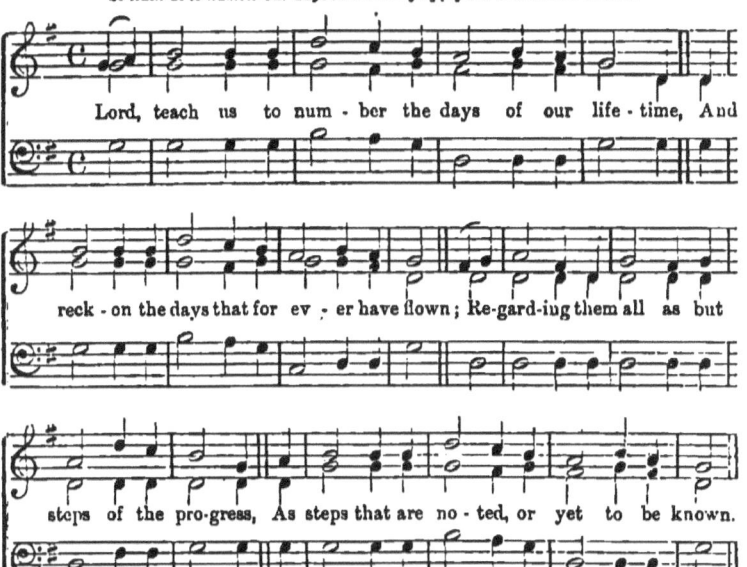

Lord, teach us to num - ber the days of our life - time, And reck - on the days that for ev - er have flown; Re-gard-ing them all as but steps of the pro-gress, As steps that are no - ted, or yet to be known.

2.

Yes! Life is the name of that slender existence
That dwells in the perishing body of clay;
A flow'r of the morning, it grows in the sunshine—
It blooms for a little, and dies in a day.

3.

Time passes unheeded and often forgotten,
The chimes of the seasons go merrily round;
The dread hour of midnight steals on in the dark ess,
And thunders the night-watch with dull, heavy sound.

4.

The wave of the ripple that rises from ocean,
Speeds onwards and dances, from bond-age set free,
Till, swollen with fulness, its period exhausted,
It gently retires to the depths of the sea.

5.

The dew of the night and the mist of the morning
Scarce live but a moment, when upward they fly.
The babe of our joy is the child of our sorrow;
To-day it is fondled—to-morrow to die.

6.

Then teach us to number the days of our lifetime,
And study to walk in more heave ly ways:
As we reckon the hours and the chimes of the noontide,
So teach us, great Teacher, to number our days.

Children of Jerusalem. 7's.

No. 90   *" Hosanna to the Son of David."*   KILLARNEY.

1. Chil-dren of Je - ru - sa - lem Sang the praise of Je - sus' name. Chil-dren, too, of mo - dern days, Join to sing the Saviour's praise. Hark! hark! hark! while infant voices sing, Hark! hark! hark! while infant voices sing Loud ho-san-nas, loud ho-san nas, loud ho-san - nas to our King.

2.	3.
We are taught to love the Lord ;	Parents, teachers, old and young,
We are taught to read his word ;	All unite to swell the song :
We are taught the way to heaven ;	Higher, and yet higher rise,
Praise for all to God be given.	Till hosannas reach the skies.
Hark, &c.	Hark, &c.

Glorious Things.*

No. 91.

T. C. O'KANE.

"Glorious things of thee are spoken."

Cheerful.

1. Glo-rious things of thee are spoken, Zi-on, cit-y of our God!
2. See the streams of liv-ing waters, Springing from eter-nal love,
3. Round each habi-ta-tion hov'ring, See the fire and cloud ap-pear,

He whose word can not be broken, Formed thee for his own abode.
Still sup-ply our sons and daughters, And all fear of want remove.
For a glo-ry and a cov'ring, Showing that the Lord is near.

On the Rock of A-ges founded What can shake thy sure repose?
Who can faint while such a riv-er Ev-er flows our thirst t'assuage?
He who gives us dai-ly manna, He who list-ens when we cry!

With sal-va-tion's walls sur-rounded, Thou may'st smile at all thy foes.
Grace, which like the Lord the giv-er, Nev-er fails from age to age.
Let him hear our loud ho-sanna, Ris-ing to his throne on high.

* Specially contributed by the author of "FRESH LEAVES."

No. 92   ## Call to Praise.   ENGLISH.

"Praise him with string instruments and organs: let everything that hath breath, praise the Lord."

1. Come, O come, with sa-cred lays, Let us sound th' Al-migh-ty's praise !

Hi-ther bring, in true con - sent, Heart, and voice, and in - stru - ment.

To your voic - es tune the lute; Let not tongue nor string be mute;

Not a crea-ture dumb be found, That hath ei - ther voice or sound.

2 Let such things as do not live,
In still music praises give :
Lowly pipe, all ye that creep
On the earth or in the deep ;
Birds, your warbling treble sing :
Clouds, your peals of thunder ring ;
Sun and moon, exalted higher,
And you, stars, augment the choir.

3 Come, ye sons of human race,
In this chorus take your place ;
And amid this mortal throng
Be ye masters of the song.

Let, in praise of God, the sound
Run a never-ending round ;
That our holy hymn may be
Everlasting, as is he.

4 So shall he, from heaven's high tower,
On the earth his blessing shower ;
All this huge wide orb we see
Shall one choir, one temple be.
Then our voices we will rear,
Till we fill it everywhere.
Come, O come, with sacred lays,
Let us sound the Almighty's praise !

Holy Child Jesus. C.M.

No. 93

Rev. W. Jones.

" Hosanna in the highest ! "

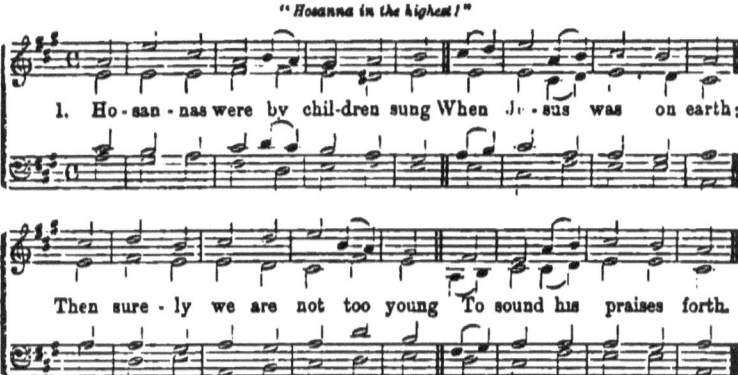

1. Ho-san-nas were by chil-dren sung When Je-sus was on earth:

Then sure-ly we are not too young To sound his praises forth.

2.
The Lord is great, the Lord is good ;
He feeds us from his store,
With earthly and with heavenly food;
We'll praise him evermore.

3.
We thank him for his gracious word ;
We thank him for his love ;
We'll sing the praises of our Lord,
Who reigns in heaven above.

No. 94

1.
THE race that long in darkness walk'd,
Have seen a glorious light ;
The people dwell in day, who dwelt
In death's surrounding night.

2.
To hail Thy rise, Thou better Sun,
The gathering nations come,
Joyous, as when the reapers bear
The harvest treasures home.

3.
For unto us a Child is born ;
To us a Son is given ;
Him shall the tribes of earth obey,
Him, all the hosts of heaven.

4.
His name shall be the Prince of Peace,
For evermore adored,
The Wonderful, the Counsellor,
The Great and Mighty Lord.

No. 95

1.
COME, children, hail the Prince of Peace,
Obey the Saviour's call ;
Come, seek his face, and taste his grace :
And crown him Lord of all.

2.
Ye lambs of Christ, your tribute bring,
Ye children great and small ;
Hosannas sing to Christ your King,
And crown him Lord of all.

3.
This Jesus will your sins forgive,
For such he drank the gall,
For such he died, that they might live
To crown him Lord of all.

4.
Let all these children, Lord, be thine ;
Save them from Satan's thrall ;
Then we shall meet at Jesu's feet,
To crown him Lord of all.

Thanksgiving Hymn.

No. 96

"It is good to give thanks unto the Lord."

J. A. P. SCHULER.

1. We plough the fertile meadows, And sow the furrow'd land, But yet the waving harvest
Depends on God's own hand; It is his mercy gives us The sunshine and the rain;
That paints in verdant beauty The mountain and the plain. Ev'ry blessing we en-joy
Comes to us from God. Then praise his name, For he is e-ver good,

2.

By him were all things fashioned,
  Around us and afar ;
He made the earth and ocean,
  And ev'ry shining star ;
He made the pleasant spring-time
  The summer bright and warm,
The golden days of autumn,
  The winter, and the storm.
        Ev'ry blessing, &c.

3.

He makes the glorious sun set,
  The moon to sail on high ;
He bids the breezes fan us,
  And thund'ring clouds to fly ;
He gives us ev'ry blessing ;
  To him our lives we owe ;
He sent his Son to save us
  From sin, and death, and woe.
        Ev'ry blessing, &c.

Delight in God.

No. 97

Dr. Thomas Hastings.

" Thy commandments are my delight.

Quick.

1. De - light in the Lord, With sweet-est ac - cord, All ye who are free - ly for - given; Him - self he once of - fered, For sin - ners he suf - fered To o - pen the por- tals of heaven.

2 Delight in the Lord,
His wonders record,
Whose name is Almighty to save;
His own resurrection
Brought death in subjection,
Abolished the power of the grave.

3 Delight in the Lord,
Confide in his word,
Our Prophet, our Priest, and our King;

His wisdom, his merit,
His guidance, his spirit,
His love we exultingly sing.

4 Delight in the Lord,
In his sceptre and sword,
His foes shall assail him in vain;
His kingdom all glorious
Will soon rise victorious,
O'er all the wide world he shall reign.

The New Best Name.

No. 98

PHILIP PHILLIPS.

"To him that overcometh will I give to eat of the hidden manna, and will give him a white stone, and in the stone a new name written, which no man knoweth saving he that receiveth it."

1. He hath giv'n me a gem, as a
3. And oft when my day-dreams draw

to-ken so rare, In my bo-som I've placed it for safe-keep-ing
nigh to a close, And I sigh for the calm of the evening's re-

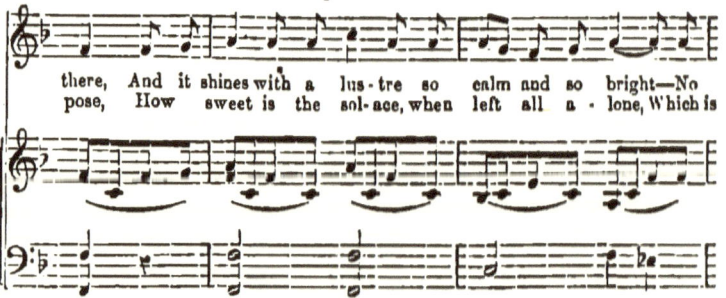

there, And it shines with a lus-tre so calm and so bright—No
pose, How sweet is the sol-ace, when left all a-lone, Which is

drift from the mountain was ev - er so white. 2. This em - blem of
mine when I gaze on my beau - ti - ful stone. 4. And this blest bond of

pu - ri - ty bears my new name, Which no one can read, tho' to
u - nion is promis'd the same To all who will love, and be -

Follow the voice.

me 'tis so plain; And I hope to preserve it as long as I
lieve on his name; Ah! who would not cov - et a to - ken so

live, For so pre - cious a gift none, but Je - sus can give.
rare, In their bo - som to place it for safe - keep-ing there.

Praise the Lord!

No. 99   Stoel.

"My lips shall praise Thee."

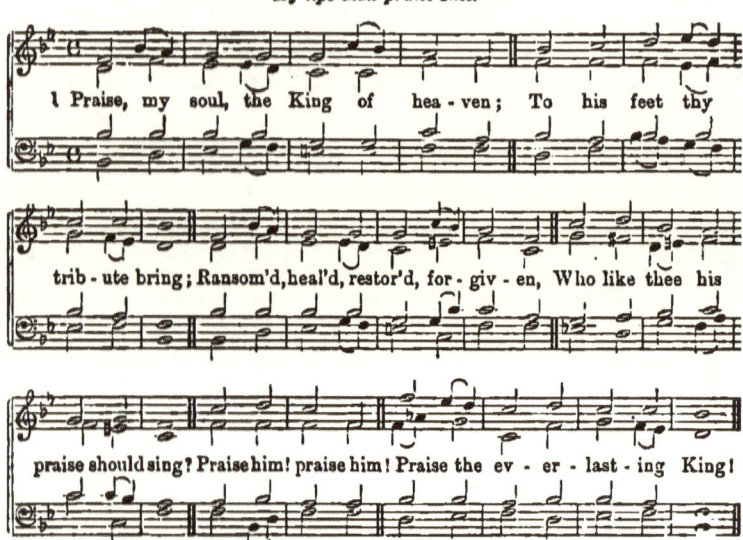

1 Praise, my soul, the King of hea - ven; To his feet thy trib - ute bring; Ransom'd, heal'd, restor'd, for - giv - en, Who like thee his praise should sing? Praise him! praise him! Praise the ev - er - last - ing King!

2.

Praise him for his grace and favour
To our fathers in distress;
Praise him still the same for ever,
Slow to chide, and swift to bless.
    Praise him! Praise him!
Glorious in his faithfulness!

3.

Angels, help us to adore him,
Ye behold him face to face!
Sun and moon bow down before him,
Dwellers all in time and space,
    Praise him! Praise him!
Praise with us the God of grace!

No. 100

1.

LET us now, with hearts united,
  Seek and praise our God above;
Far too long we him have slighted:
But if now we seek his love,
    We shall find him,
And our souls he will approve.

2

If we seek him through the Saviour,
Pleading all he did below,

We shall surely find his favour,
  And be saved from endless woe;
    And to heaven
After death our souls will go.

3.

If we seek his Holy Spirit
In our young and early days,
He will grant, through Jesus' merit,
  Rich supplies of heavenly grace:
    And will fit us
For eternal songs of praise.

No. 101 ## Confess the Lord. P.M.

" That every tongue should confess that Jesus Christ is Lord.

1. { Migh-ty God, while an-gels bless thee, May we chil-dren speak thy name ?
   { Lord of men as well as an-gels, Thou art ev - 'ry crea-ture's theme !

2. { Lord of ev - 'ry land and na - tion, An-cient of e - ter - nal days !
   { Sounded through the wide cre-a - tion Be thy just and law - ful praise.

Hal - le - lu - jah, hal - le - lu - jah, hal - le - lu - jah, A - - - men.

Hal - le - lu - jah, hal - le - lu - jah, hal - le - lu - jah, A - - - men.

3.
Brightness of the Father's glory,
Shall thy praise unuttered lie ?
Flee my tongue such guilty silence,
Sing the Lord who came to die,
    Hallelujah, etc.

4.
From the highest throne in glory,
To the cross of deepest woe,—
All to ransom guilty captives ;
Flow, my praise, for ever flow.
    Hallelujah, etc.

No. 102

1.
WHY did Jesus come from heaven,
    Live a suffering life, and die ?
'Twas that we might be forgiven,
And hereafter live on high.
    Let us praise him,
Now he reigns above the sky.

2.
Jesus is the only Saviour ;
All our hope from Jesus springs ;
Jesus is the world's Redeemer ;
Lord of lords and King of kings.
    Let us praise him,
For his grace salvation brings.

3.
Jesus kindly will receive us,
Who to him for refuge flee ;
Jesus never can deceive us ;
Our unchanging friend is he.
    Let us praise him :
From our sins he sets us free.

4.
May we know his full salvation,
And, when this short life is o'er
Reach that heavenly habitation,
Whither he is gone before.
    May we praise him,
In his kingdom evermore.

No. 103   **America.** (National Hymn.)   CAREY.
19th P.M. 6's & 4's.

"The Lord shall give his people the blessing of peace."

Maestoso.

1. My country, 'tis of thee, Sweet land of lib-er-ty, Of thee I sing; Land where my

fathers died, Land of the pilgrim's pride, From ev'ry mountain side Let freedom ring.

2 My native country! thee,
Land of the noble free,
　Thy name I love;
I love thy rocks and rills,
Thy woods and templed hills;
My heart with rapture thrills,
　Like that above.

3 Let music swell the breeze,
And ring from all the trees
　Sweet freedom's song:

Let mortal tongues awake,
Let all that breathe partake,
Let rocks their silence break,
　The sound prolong.

4 Our father's God, to thee—
Author of liberty,
　To thee we sing:
Long may our land be bright
With freedom's holy light;
Protect us by thy might,
　Great God, our King.

No. 104

GOD bless our native land!
　Firm may she ever stand,
Through storm and night;
When the wild tempests rave,
Ruler of winds and wave,
Do thou our country save
　By thy great might.

2 For her our prayer shall rise
To God above the skies;
　On him we wait:
Thou who art ever nigh,
Guarding with watchful eye,
To thee aloud we cry,
　God save the State!

No. 105

COME, thou Almighty King,
　Help us thy name to sing,
Help us to praise:
Father all glorious,
O'er all victorious,
Come and reign over us,
　Ancient of days.

2 Jesus, our Lord, arise,
Scatter our enemies.
　And make them fall;
Let thine almighty aid
Our sure defence be made;
Our souls on thee be stay'd:
　Lord, hear our call.

3 Come, thou incarnate Word,
Gird on thy mighty sword,
　Our prayer attend;
Come, and thy people bless,
And give thy word success.
Spirit of holiness,
　On us descend.

4 To the great One in Three
Eternal praises be
　Hence, evermore.
His sovereign majesty
May we in glory see,
And to eternity
　Love and adore.

Our Country.

No. 106   *" A land that floweth with milk and honey."*   PHILIP PHILLIPS.

1. Our country, un ri-valled in beau - ty And splendour that cannot be told, . . How
2. Our country, the birthplace of free-dom, The land where our forefathers trod, . . And

lovely thy hills and thy woodlands, Arrayed in a sunlight of gold. The eagle, proud king of the
sang in the aisles of the forest Their hymn of thanksgiving to God. Their bark they had moored in the

mountain,   Is soar-ing, ma-jes - tic and free; Thy ri-vers and lakes in their grandeur,
bar-bour,   No more on the o - cean to roam; And there, in the wilds of New Eng land,

Roll on to the arms of the sea, . . . Roll on to the arms of the sea. .
They foun-ded a coun-try and home, . . They found-ed a coun-try and home. .

3.
Our country, the past, and its glory,
  Still honour the names of the dead;
The statesman that crowned thee with laurel,
  The he oes and veterans that bled.
Mount Vernon, where Washington slumbers,
  The soul of thy freedom for years,
A willow droops tenderly o er him,
  Go hallow his grave with thy tears.

4.
Our country with ardent devotion,
  In God may thy children abide;
In him be the strength of our nation,
  His laws and its counsel its guide.
Our banner—that time-honoured banner
  That floats o'er the ocean's bright foam—
God keep them unsullied for ever—
  Our standard, our union, our home.

Thou Great Creator

No. 107   ALFRED SMITH.

"Remember now thy Creator in the days of thy youth."

1. Thou great Cre - a - tor, sov'reign Lord, To thee my voice I raise,

With ho - ly zeal my heart in-spire, And tune my soul to praise.

Thy word my on - ly com - fort still, My ref - uge day by day:

Oh, let me trust it, gra-cious Lord, And ev - er watch and pray.

2.

My cup with joy thy goodness fills,
  Thy mercy I adore ;
Oh, give me strength and grace divine,
  To love thee more and more.
With humble faith and earnest hope,
  Where'er my path may be,
I'll strive to run the heavenly race,
  And look for help to thee.

3.

And when beside the rolling waves
  Of Jordan's stream I stand,
Dear Saviour, thou wilt bear me then
  To Canaan's promised land :
There with the joyful host above,
  My raptured voice I'll raise,
When faith, and prayer, and hope are lost
  In our *glad song of praise.*

Part III.]   [Price 10 cents each. $8 per 100.

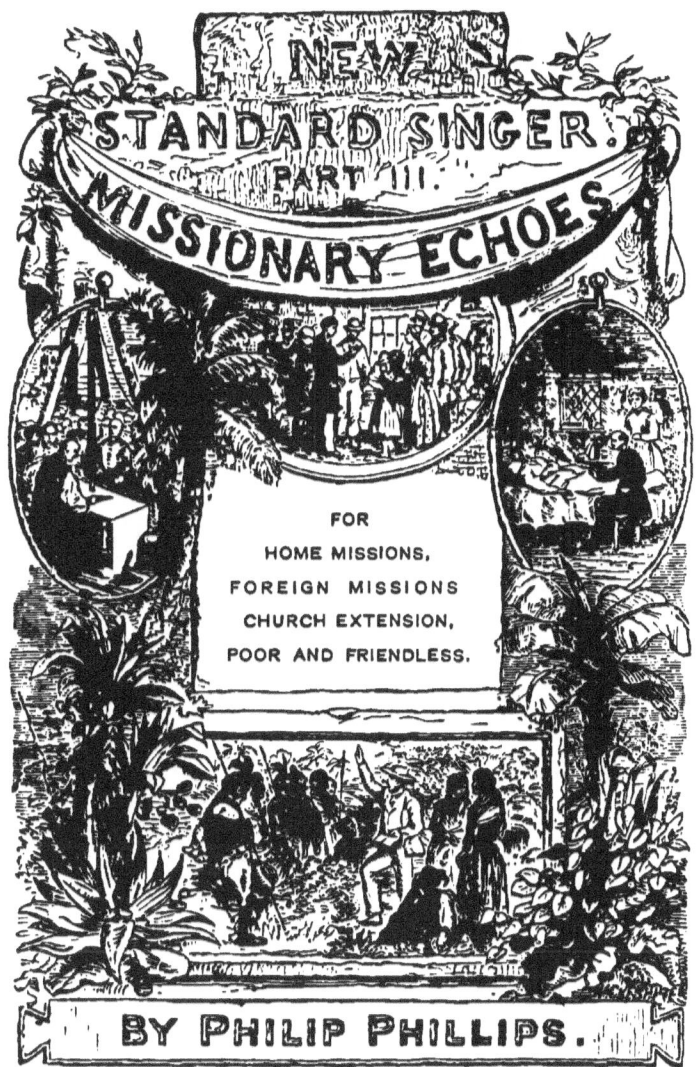

NEW STANDARD SINGER.
PART III.
MISSIONARY ECHOES

FOR

HOME MISSIONS,

FOREIGN MISSIONS

CHURCH EXTENSION,

POOR AND FRIENDLESS.

BY PHILIP PHILLIPS.

PHILIP PHILLIPS, Author and Publisher,
805 Broadway, New York.

HITCHCOCK & WALDEN,
Cincinnati, Chicago, and St. Louis.

Our Field is the World.

No. 108.   PHILLIPS AND O'KANE.

"Lo! I am with you alway, even unto the end of the world."

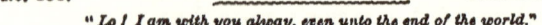

1. Dis - ci - ples of Jesus, why stand ye here idle? Go work in his vineyard, he calls us to-day;
2. Our field is the world, and our work is before us, To each is ap-pointed a message to bear;

The night is approaching when no man can labor, Our Master commands us, and shall we delay?
At home or abroad, in the cottage or palace, Wherev- er di- rected our mis-sion is there.

CHORUS.

Our field is the world! Our field is the world! Look up, for the har - vest is near;

When the reapers from glory Will shout as they come, And the Lord of the vineyard appear.

3.
Perhaps we are called from the highways
   and hedges,
To gather the lowly, despised, and
   oppressed ;
It this be our duty, then why should we
   falter ?
We'll do it, and trust to our Saviour
   the rest.
   Our field is the world, etc.

4.
Instead of the thorn shall the myrtle be
   planted ;
The desert shall blossom and bloom as
   the rose ;
The palm tree rejoicing shall spread forth
   her branches ;
The lamb and the lion together repose.
   Our field is the world, etc.

No. 109   ## Macedonian Cry.   Arr. by Philip Phillips

"Come over into Macedonia, and help us."

1 Yes, my na-tive land, I love thee; All thy scenes, I love them well;

Friends, connections, hap-py coun-try! Can I bid you all fare-well?

Can I leave you? Can I leave you, Far in hea-then lands to dwell?

No 110

2 Yes, I hasten from you gladly,
  From the scenes I loved so well—
Far away, ye billows, bear me ;
Lovely native land, farewell !
  Pleased I leave thee,
  Far in heathen lands to dwell.

3 In the desert let me labour ;
  On the mountains let me tell
How he died—the blessed Saviour—
To redeem a world from hell !
  Let me hasten,
  Far in heathen lands to dwell.

4 Bear me on, thou restless ocean ;
  Let the winds my canvas swell—
Heaves my heart with warm emotion,
While I go far hence to dwell.
  Glad I bid thee,
  Native land, Farewell ! farewell !

G O, ye heralds of salvation,
  Go, proclaim " Redeeming blood ,"
Publish to that barb'rous nation,
Peace and pardon from our God ;
  Tell the heathen,
  None but Christ can do them good.

2 Distant tho' our souls are blending,
  Still our hearts are warm and true ;
In our prayers to heav'n ascending,
Brethren, we'll remember you ;
  Heav'n preserve you
  Safely all your journey through.

3 When your mission here is finish'd,
  And your work on earth is done,
May your souls, by grace replenish'd,
Find acceptance thro' the Son !
  Thence admitted,
  Dwell for ever near his throne.

God with Us.

No. 111

PHILIP PHILLIPS.

"Hitherto hath the Lord helped us."

1, Lo! our fa-thers' God is with us! We can trace his migh-ty hand,

In our churches, vast in num-ber, Wide ex - tend - ing o'er our land.

Let our full u - nit - ed cho - rus E - ver on - ward roll a - long,

ritard.

And the year of time be vo - cal With our loud, ecs - ta - tic song.

ritard.

GOD WITH US—*continued.*

CHORUS, BY WM. B. BRADBURY.—*Full and loud.*

March-ing a-long, we are marching a-long; Ris-ing and progressing, we are march-ing a-long; Our hearts are u - nit - ed, and this be our song: Our fa - thers' God is with us while we're march - ing a - long.

2.

Lo! our fathers' God is with us!
Lost in wonder, we adore
Him who brought them safely hither
With the Gospel to our shore.
Fired with zeal, and armed with courage,
Strong in faith and love divine,
Thro' the darkest cloud that gathered
They could see his glory shine.
Marching along, &c.

3.

Lo! our fathers' God is with us!
They have laid their armour down,
They have passed the vale of shadow,
Left the cross to wear the crown:

We must bear their glorious standard,
Wield our veteran fathers' sword,
In the army of the faithful
We are battling for the Lord.
Marching along, &c.

4.

Lo! our fathers' God is with us!
Sing aloud with heart and voice,
Still increasing and progressing,
Brethren, let us all rejoice!
Hallelujah! what a meeting,
When we reach the shining shore,
There with saints who've gone before us,
Shout "Free grace" for evermore!
Marching along, &c.

How He Loves Us.

No. 112.   C. H. Bateman.

" He was bruised for our iniquities."

1. Bound up - on th'ac-cursed tree, Faint and bleeding, who is he? See his eyes so

pale and dim, Streaming blood, and writhing limb; See the flesh with scourges torn;

See the crown of twist-ed thorn; See the drooping death-dew'd brow;

Son of man,'tis thou! 'tis thou!

2 Bound-upon th' accursed tree,
Dread and awful, who was he?
Though his lifeless corpse was laid
In a cold sepulchral bed,
Soon the Saviour from the grave
Rose a conqu'ror strong to save;
Bright the crown that decks his brow—
Son of God, 'tis thou! 'tis thou!

Work while 'tis Day.

No. 113.   T. C. O'Kane.

" The night cometh, when no man can work."

1. Work, for the night is coming; Work thro' the morning hours; Work while the dew is

WORK WHILE 'TIS DAY—*continued.*

spark - ling; Work 'mid springing flow'rs; Work when the day grows bright - er;

Work in the glowing sun; Work, for the night is com-ing, When man's work is done.

Work when the day grows bright - er; Work in the glowing sun;

Work when the day grows brighter; Work in the glow-ing

Work, for the night is com' - ing, When man's work is done.

sun, for the night is com ing, When man's work is done.

2.

Work, for the night is coming;
  Work through the sunny noon:
Fill brightest hours with labour;
  Rest comes sure and soon.
Give every flying minute
  Something to keep in store;
Work, for the night is coming,
  When man works no more.

3.

Work, for the night is coming,
  Under the sunset skies;
While their bright tints are glowing,
  Work, for daylight flies.
Work till the last beam fadeth,
  Fadeth to shine no more:
Work while the night is dark'ning,
  When man's work is o'er.

Cheerful Giver.

No. 114

PHILIP PHILLIPS.

" God loveth the cheerful giver."

1. Give! give! give! Give of the fruits of thy labour; Give of thy "basket and

store;" Give to the cause of the needy Jesus will give to thee more.

CHORUS.

God lov-eth the cheerful giver, 'Tis one of his sa-cred laws;

He will bless your alms when rightly given, To the glo-ry of his cause.

2.	3.
Give! give! give!	Give! give! give!
Give to the pilgrim and stranger,	Give to distribute the Bible
Lighten their burden of care;	Over the isles of the sea;
Give to the widow and orphan,	Nations now sitting in darkness
Help them their sorrow to bear.	Light from its pages will see.
God loveth, etc.	God loveth, etc.

The Reaping Time. 7s.

No. 115   Rev. R. Lowry.

"A time to be born, and a time to die."

1. Je - sus, we thy lambs would be,   Humbly would we fol - low thee;
2. Now the field with grain is white,   Now the day is dawn-ing bright;

Wait - ing for the joy - ful day,   When all care will pass a - way.
Bright - er far the sky will be,   When the Mas- ter we shall see.

CHORUS.

When the reap-ing time shall come, And an - gels shout the har-vest home.

When the reaping time shall come, And an- gels shout the har-vest home.

3 May we wait, and watch, and pray,
For the coming of that day,
When the wheat shall sifted be,
And the chaff be driven from thee!
   When the reaping, &c.

No. 116
1 Swiftly pass the seasons round;
Constant change on earth is found,
We are fading day by day,
And must shortly pass away.
   When the reaping, &c.

2 Time once lost returns no more:
Time with us will soon be o'er;
Oh, may we be early wise,
To improve it as it flies.
   When the reaping, &c.

3 Help us, Lord, to seek thy face
Daily may we grow in grace,
Till we rise to dwell above,
In the kingdom of thy love.
   When the reaping, &c.

6

Come, ye Disconsolate. 30th P.M.

No. 117   S. WEBBE

" God is our refuge and strength : a very present help in trouble."

SOLO, DUET, OR TRIO.

1. Come, ye dis - con - so-late, where'er ye lan - guish,
Come to the mer - cy seat, Fer - vent - ly kneel;

1ST TIME DUET, 2ND TIME CHORUS.

Here bring your wounded hearts, Here tell your an - guish;

Earth has no sor - row that heav'n can - not heal.

2.

Joy of the desolate, light of the straying,
  Hope of the penitent, fadeless and
    pure ; —
Here speaks the Comforter, tenderly
  saying—
    Earth has no sorrow that heav'n
  cannot cure.

3.

Here see the bread of life; see waters flowing
  Forth from the throne of God, pure
    from above ;
Come to the feast of love; come, ever
  knowing—
    Earth has no sorrow but heav'n can
  remove.

Labour for Christ.

No. 118

"The harvest truly is plenteous, but the labourers are few."

1. For Je-sus our Saviour, our talent, our time, Our substance we'll cheerfully spend ;

Whatever our lot, and wherever our clime, We'll labour and love to the end. . We'll

CHORUS.

labour and love to the end. O yes, we'll do all that we can ; O yes, we'll do all that we

can. The harvest is great, and the labourers are few, Then we will do all that we can.

2

And if we have only a penny to give,
  We'll give it, though scanty our store,
For they who give nothing when little they have,
  When wealthy, will give little more.
          Chorus.

3.

But if an abundance we have at command,
  O Father, the Spirit bestow,

To scatter our wealth with a liberal hand,
  And succour the children of woe.
          Chorus.

4.

Though God may not call us in regions afar,
  To scatter the Gospel abroad,
We'll point these around us to Bethlehem's star
  To Heaven, to Home, and to God.
          Chorus.

The Promised Time.

No. 119

"And the desert shall rejoice and blossom as the rose."

Animated.

1. Re - joice, re - joice, the promised time is com - ing, Re - joice, re -
D. C. Re - joice, re - joice, the promised time is com - ing, Re - joice, re -

joice, the wil - der - ness shall bloom, And Zi - on's chil - dren
joice, the wil - der - ness shall bloom.

then shall sing, "The des - erts all are blossom - ing:" Re - joice, Re -

- joice, the promised time is com - ing, Re - joice, re - joice, the

wil - der - ness shall bloom; The Gos - pel ban - ner, wide unfurl'd, Shall

wave in tri - umph o'er the world; And ev - ery crea - ture,

bond and free, Shall hail the glo - rious ju - bi - lee.

2.

Rejoice, rejoice, the promised time is coming,
  Rejoice, rejoice, Jerusalem shall sing;
From Zion shall the law go forth,
And all shall hear from south to north:
Rejoice, rejoice, the promised time is coming,
  Rejoice, rejoice, Jerusalem shall sing;
And truth shall sit on every hill,
And blessings flow in every rill,
And praise shall every heart employ,
And every voice shall shout with joy:
Rejoice, rejoice, the promised time is coming,
  Rejoice, rejoice, Jerusalem shall sing.

3.

Rejoice, rejoice, the promised time is coming,
  Rejoice, rejoice, the Prince of Peace shall reign,
And lambs shall with the leopard play,
For nought shall harm in Zion's way:
Rejoice, rejoice, the promised time is coming,
  Rejoice, rejoice, the Prince of Peace shall reign.
The sword and spear of needless worth,
Shall prune the tree and plow the earth,
And peace shall smile from shore to shore,
And nations shall learn war no more:
Rejoice, rejoice, the promised time is coming,
  Rejoice, rejoice, the Prince of Peace shall reign.

Gospel Victory.

No. 120

" Come over into Macedonia and help us."

PHILIP PHILLIPS.

1. Go, sound the trump from India's shore, And bid the Hin-doo weep no more,

rit. *pp*   *a tempo.*

Hin-doo weep no more; From i - dols vain, and Gan-ges' wave, The

rit. *pp*   Cho.   *tempo.* *ff*

low-ly Saviour comes to save, comes to save, From tyrant's power and

ff

Satan's sway, The Gospel gives the vic-to-ry ! vic-to-ry ! vic-to-ry !

2 Go, sound the trump on Afric's shore,
And bid the |: natives weep no more !:|
From cruel chains, and bloody grave,
The lowly Saviour |: comes to save. :|—From tyrant's, &c.

3 Go, sound the trump on Judah's shore,
And say to |: Israel weep no more !:|
The Lord of glory, slain by you,
Will yet restore the |: guilty Jew. :|—From tyrant's, &c.

4 Go, sound the trump on every shore,
And bid poor |: sinners weep no more !:|
The blood that flowed from Jesus' veins
Will wash away your |: crimson stains. :|—From tyrant's, &c.

Jesus Invites Me.

No. 121

PHILIP PHILLIPS.

" The Lord thinketh upon me."

1. Je - sus invites me! Je - sus invites me! Kind in - vi - ta - tion all
2. Who can condemn me, who can condemn me; Je - sus has died, and my

doubts to remove; Gracious his par-don, precious his blessing, Boundless the
sins are forgiv'n; Come then, poor sinner, put on the vestment—Put on the

wealth of Redeem- ing Love. Ne'er did a fountain,—ne'er did Bethes - da,—
breast-plate and gaze up to heav'n. Cast off thy fears then—raise " E- ben- e - zer,"

Ne'er did the Jor - dan's pure cleansing flood, Bear on their wa-ters a
List to the joys of the an - gels a - bove; Lo! this their song—here's one

vir - tue so heal - ing, As Je - sus' all precious, a - ton - ing blood.
sin - ner re - pent - ing, Bound - less the wealth of " Re- deem - ing Love."

No. 122   Consider the Poor.

"For ye have the poor with ye always, and whensoever ye will ye can do them good."

Words by Wm. Edsall.   Philip Phillips.

1. Re - member the poor, the des - o - late poor, Nor leave them to
2. Re - member the poor, be kind to the heart, So pa - tient - ly
3. Re - member the poor, for hard is their lot; Go, vis - it the

wan - der from door to door; Be read - y and will - ing your
try - ing to bear its part; The wid - ow who toils by the
hum - ble and lone - ly cot; When blest is your bask - et, and

comforts to share With those who are burdened with sor - row and care.
em - bers that wane, While tears from her eye - lids are fall - ing like rain.
prospered your store, Be grate - ful to God, and re - mem - ber the poor.

CHORUS.

For the promise is sure, The promise is sure; Blessed is he,

Repeat pp.

Bless - ed is he, Bless - ed is he that con - si - d'reth the poor.

No. 123

O Happy Land.

ALFRED SMITH.

" Here are they that keep the commandments of God."

1. O hap - py land! O hap - py land! Where saints and an-gels dwell;

We long to join that glo-rious band, And all their anthems swell.

But ev - ery voice in yon- der throng On earth has breathed a prayer;

No lips untaught may join that song, Or learn the mu - sic there.

2.

Thou heavenly Friend, thou heavenly Friend,
O hear us when we pray ;
Now let thy pardoning grace descend,
And take our sins away.
Be all our fresh, our youthful days,
To thy blest service given ;
Then we shall meet to sing thy praise,
A ransomed band in heaven.

No. 124   **Duke Street. L.M.**   J. HATTON

" Praise ye the Lord, for it is good to sing praises unto our God."

1.   From all that dwell be-low the skies, Let the Cre-a-tor's praise a-rise.
2.   E-ter-nal are thy mer-cies, Lord; E-ter-nal truth at-tends thy word.

Let the Re-deem-er's name be sung, Through every land, by ev-ery tongue.
Thy praise shall sound from shore to shore, Till suns shall rise and set no more.

3.	4.
Your lofty themes, ye mortals, bring ;	In every land begin the song ;
In songs of praise divinely sing ;	To every land the strains belong :
The great salvation loud proclaim,	In cheerful sounds all voices raise,
And shout for joy the Saviour's name.	And fill the world with loudest praise.

No. 125

1.

SOON may the last glad song arise,
   Thro' all the millions of the skies—
That song of triumph which records
That all the earth is now the Lord's.

2.

Let thrones, and powers, and kingdoms, be
Obedient, mighty God, to thee ;
And over land, and stream, and main,
Now wave the sceptre of thy reign.

3.

O let that glorious anthem swell ;
Let host to host the triumph tell, .
Till not one rebel heart remains,
But over all the Saviour reigns.

No. 126

1.

JESUS ! thy church, with longing eyes,
   For thine expected coming waits ,
When will the promised light arise,
And glory beam on Zion's gates ?

2.

O come and reign o'er every land ,
Let Satan from his throne be hurled,
All nations bow to thy command,
And grace revive a dying world.

3.

Teach us in watchfulness and prayer,
To wait for thine appointed hour ;
And fit us, by thy grace, to share
The triumphs of thy conqu'ring power.

No. 127 **Lenox.** **3rd P.M.** Edsou.

" O clap your hands together, all ye people, O sing unto God with the voice of melody."

1. Blow ye the trumpet, blow, The gladly-solemn sound; Let all the nations know,

To earth's re - mo'est bound,   The year of ju - bi - lee is come,

The year of ju - bi - lee is come ; Re-turn, ye ransom'd sin - ners,   home.

2 Jesus. our great High Priest,
  Hath full atonement made ;
  Ye weary spirits, rest;
  Ye mournful souls, be glad :
The year of jubilee is come ;
Return, ye ransomed sinners, home.

3 Extol the Lamb of God,—
  The all-atoning Lamb ;
  Redemption in his blood
  Throughout the world proclaim :
The year of jubilee is come ;
Return, ye ransomed sinners, home.

4 Ye slaves of sin and hell,
  Your liberty receive,
  And safe in Jesus dwell,
  And blest in J sus live :
The year of jubilee is come ;
Return ye ransomed sinners, home.

5 Ye who have sold for nought
  Your heritage above,
  Shall have it back unbought,
  The gift of Jesus' love :
The year of jubilee is come ;
Return, ye ransomed sinners, home.

No. 128

GOD is gone up on high,
    With a triumphant noise,—
  The clarions of the sky
  Proclaim th' angelic joys :
Join all on earth, rejoice and sing ;
Glory ascribe to glory's King.

2 All power to our great Lord
  Is by the Father given :
  By angel hosts adored,
  He reigns supreme in heaven :
Join all on earth, rejoice and sing :
Glory ascribe to glory s King.

3 High on his holy seat,
  He bears the righteous sway ;
  His foes beneath his feet
  Shall sink and die away :
Join all ou earth, rejoice and sing;
Glory ascribe to glory's King.

4 Till all the earth, renew'd
  In righteousness divine,
  With all the hosts of God,
  In one great chorus join,
Join all on earth, rejoice and sing;
Glory ascribe to glory's King.

No. 129   # Webb.   26th P.M.   G. J. Webb.

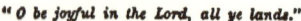

" O be joyful in the Lord, all ye lands."

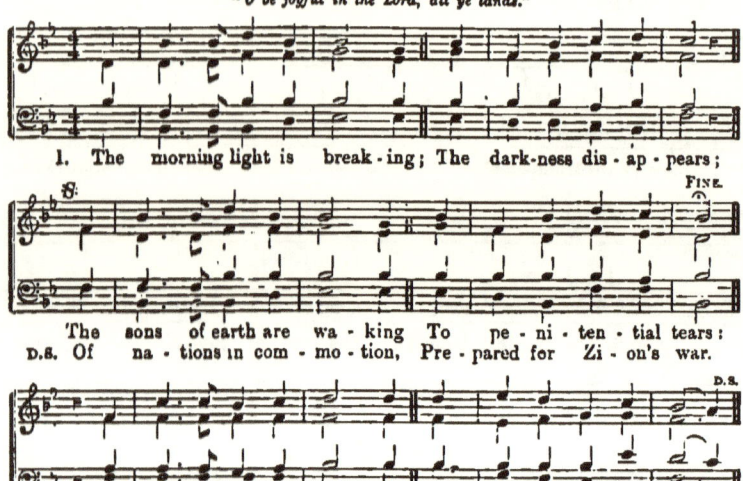

1. The morning light is break - ing ; The dark-ness dis - ap - pears ;

The sons of earth are wa - king To pe - ni - ten - tial tears :
D.S. Of na - tions in com - mo - tion, Pre - pared for Zi - on's war.

Each breeze that sweeps the o - cean Brings tidings from a - far,

2 See heathen nations bending
  Before the God we love,
And thousand hearts ascending
  In gratitude above ;
While sinners, now confessing,
  The gospel call obey,
And seek the Saviour's blessing,—
  A nation in a day.

3 Blest river of salvation,
  Pursue thy onward way ;
Flow thou to every nation,
  Nor in thy richness stay :
Stay not till all the lowly
  Triumphant reach their home :
Stay not till all the holy
  Proclaim—"The Lord is come !"

No. 130

WHEN shall the voice of singing
  Flow joyfully along ?
When hill and valley, ringing
  With one triumphant song,
Proclaim the contest ended,
  And him who once was slain,
Again to earth descended,
  In righteousness to reign.

2 Then from the craggy mountains
  The sacred shout shall fly ;
And shady vales and fountains
  Shall echo the reply.
High tower and lowly dwelling
  Shall send the chorus round,
All hallelujahs swelling
  In one eternal sound !

No. 131

ROLL on, thou mighty ocean ;
  And, as thy billows flow,
Bear messengers of mercy
  To every land below.
Arise, ye gales, and waft them
  Safe to the destined shore ;
That man may sit in darkness,
  And death's black shade no more.

2 Oh, thou eternal Ruler,
  Who holdest in thine arm
The tempests of the ocean,
  Protect them from all harm !
Thy presence, Lord, be with them,
  Wherever they may be ;
Though far from us who love them,
  Still let them be with thee.

No. 132   **Sessions.** L.M.   L. O. EMERSON.

" Behold I will send my messenger and he shall prepare the way before me."

1. Go preach my Gos - pel, saith the Lord,— Bid the whole world my grace receive ;
2. I'll make your great commission known ; And ye shall prove my Gospel true,
3. Teach all the na - tions my commands, I'm with you till the world shall end ;

He shall be saved who trus's my word, And he con - demn'd who won't be-lieve.
By all the works that I have done, By all the won - ders ye shall do.
All power is trusted in my hands, I can de - stroy, and I de - fend.

No. 133

BEHOLD the Christian warrior stand
In all the armour of his God ;
The Spirit's sword is in his hand,
His feet are with the Gospel shod.

2 In panoply of truth complete,
Salvation's helmet on his head ;
With righteousness, a breastplate meet,
And faith's broad shield before him
spread.

3 Undaunted to the field he goes ;
Yet vain were skill and valour there,
Unless, to foil his legion foes,
He takes the trustiest weapon, prayer.

4 Thus, strong in his Redeemer's strength,
Sin, death, and hell, he tramples down ;
Fights the good fight, and wins at length,
Through mercy, an immortal crown.

No. 134

BEHOLD, the heathen waits to know
The joy the Gospel will bestow ;
The exiled captive to receive
The freedom Jesus has to give.

2 Come, let us, with a grateful heart,
In this blest labour share a part ;
Our prayers and off'rings gladly bring
To aid the triumphs of our King.

3 Our hearts exult in songs of praise,
That we have seen these latter days,
When our Redeemer shall be known ;
Where Satan long hath held his throne.

4 Where'er his hand hath spread the
skies,
Sweet incense to his Name shall rise ;
And slave and freeman, Greek and Jew,
By sov'reign grace be form'd anew.

Missionary Hymn. 26th P.M. 7's, 6's.

No. 135   *"The harvest is the end of the world."*   DR. L. MASON.

1. From Greenland's icy mountains, From India's coral strand, Where Afric's sunny

fountains Roll down their golden sand ; From many an ancient ri - ver, From

many a palmy plain, They call us to de - liv-er Their land from error's chain.

2 What though the spicy breezes
  Blow soft o'er Ceylon's isle ;
Though every prospect pleases,
  And only man is vile :
In vain with lavish kindness
  The gifts of God are strown ;
The heathen in his blindness
  Bows down to wood and stone.

3 Shall we, whose souls are lighted
  With wisdom from on high,
Shall we to men benighted
  The lamp of life deny ?

Salvation !—O salvation !
  The joyful sound proclaim,
Till earth's remotest nation
  Has learn'd Messiah's name.

4 Waft, waft, ye winds, his story,
  And you, ye waters, roll,
Till, like a sea of glory,
  It spreads from pole to pole :
Till o'er our ransomed nature
  The Lamb for sinners slain,
Redeemer, King, Creator,
  In bliss returns to reign.

No. 136

FROM yonder Rocky Mountains,
  With summits white and cold,
From California's fountains,
  That pour down virgin gold ;
From every western prairie,
  From every mystic mound,
They call on us to carry
  The gospel's joyful sound.

2 From Oregon benighted,
  Yet tinged with morning light ;
From fertile Utah, lighted
  With radiance worse than night ;
From Aztec hill and valley,
  Just snatched away from Rome,
They bid us rally, rally,
  And to the rescue come.

3 O ! shall we close our bosoms,
  While every breath 's a cry ?
While brothers drop like blossoms,
  And there for ever die ?
Oh ! Christian, rest not, sleep not,
  But pray, and toil, and fight,
Till those who 're weeping, weep not,
  And darkness turns to light.

4 Then, when enthroned in glory,
  With Jesus' ransomed fold,
We tell love's wondrous story,
  Upon our harps of gold ;
Each effort that we 're making
  Will sweeten heaven's employ,
And every cross we're taking,
  Add rapture to its joy.

Send the Tidings. C.M.

No. 137

From French Psalter.

" He shall save his people from their sins."

1. Hark! the voice of love and mer - cy Sounds a - loud from Cal - va - ry.

See, it rends the rocks a - sun - der, Shakes the earth, and veils the sky.

"It is fi - nish'd!" Hear the dy - ing Sa - viour cry!

2

Finish'd—all the types and shadows
Of the ceremonial law!
Finish'd—all that God had promised;
Death and Hell no more shall awe;
"It is finish'd!"
Saints, from hence your comforts draw.

3.

Tune your hearts anew, ye ransom'd!
Join to sing the glorious theme;
All on earth, and all in heaven,
Join to praise the Saviours name!
Hallelujah!
Glory to the bleeding Lamb!

No. 138

1.

SOULS in heathen darkness lying,
Where no light has broken through—
Souls that Jesus bought by dying,
Whom his soul in travail knew—
Thousand voices
Call us o'er the waters blue.

2.

Christians, hearken! none has taught them
Of His love so deep and dear;
Of the precious price that bought them;
Of the nail, the thorn, the spear;
Ye who know Him,
Guide them from their darkness drear.

3.

Haste, O haste, and spread the tidings
Wide to earth's remotest strand;
Let no brother's bitter chidings
Rise against us—when we stand
In the judgment—
From some far forgotten land.

4.

Lo! the hills for harvest whiten,
All along each distant shore;
Seaward far the islands brighten,—
Light of nations! lead us o'er:
When we seek them,
Let Thy Spirit go before.

Mission Field. L.M.

No. 139

Dr. Thos. Hastings.

" The harvest truly is plenteous, but the labourers are few."

1. O thou who from thy glo-rious throne, Hast sent thy servants to pro-claim

Sal - va-tion to a world undone, And sound through all the earth thy name.

2

From Afric's burning, arid sands,
And Asia's mild, resplendent sky ;
Let converts, from the heathen lands,
As doves unto their windows fly.

3.

For all the pow'r, beneath, above,
Thy wounded hands sustain ;
Then sway the sceptre of thy love,
And let thy mercy reign.

No. 140

1.

AT length the world is opening wide
To messengers of gospel grace ;
How shall the heralds be supplied,
For all the millions of the race.

2.

Lord, let the churches rise and shine
Under the becknings of thy hand
Bid thine with hallowed zeal combine,
Obedient to thy last command.

3.

To thee, O Lord we raise our cry,
Now be thy banners wide unfurled ;
O bring the latter glories nigh ;
Set up thy kingdom through the world.

4.

Our waiting eyes are unto thee,
To thee the heritage is giv'n
O let us thy salvation see,
Make earth the vestibule of heaven.

No. 141

1.

GO, much lov'd brethren, haste and rear
The gospel standard, void of fear ;
Go, seek with joy your destin'd shore,
To view your native land no more.

2.

Yes—Christian Heroes ! go, proclaim
Salvation through Immanuel's name ;
To barren climes the tidings bear,
And plant the Rose of Sharon there.

3.

He'll shield you with a wall of fire,
With flaming zeal your breasts inspire,
Bid raging winds their fury cease,
And hush the tempests into peace.

4.

And when our labours all are o'er,
Then we shall meet to part no more ;
Meet with the blood-bought throng to fall
And crown our Jesus Lord of all !

"What are You Going to Do."*

No. 146. PHILIP PHILLIPS.

" Wherewithal shall a young man cleanse his ways," by heeding, etc. etc.

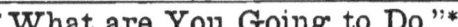

1. O what are you go-ing to do, brother? Say, what are you go-ing to do? You have

thought of some useful la- bor, But what is the end in view? You are fresh from the home of your

boy-hood, And just in the bloom of youth! Have you tast- ed the sparkling wa - ter That

CHORUS.

flows from the fount of truth? Is your heart in the Saviour's keeping? Remember he died for

you! Then what are you go-ing to do, brother? Say, what are you go- ing to do?

2. O what are you going to do, brother?
The morning of youth is past;
The vigor and strength of manhood,
My brother, are yours at last.
You are rising in worldly prospects,
And prospered in worldly things;—
A duty to those less favored,
The smile of your fortune brings.
Cho.—Go, prove that your heart is grateful—
The Lord has a work for you!
Then what are you going to do, brother?
Say, what are you going to do?

3. O what are you going to do, brother?
Your sun at its noon is high;
It shines in meridian splendor,
And rides through a cloudless sky.
You are holding a high position,
Of honor, of trust, and fame;—

Are you willing to give the glory
And praise to your Saviour's name?
Cho.—The regions that sit in darkness
Are stretching their hands to you;
Then what are you going to do, brother?
Say, what are you going to do?

4. O what are you going to do, brother?
The twilight approaches now;—
Already your locks are silvered,
And winter is on your brow.
Your talents, your time, your riches,
To Jesus, your Master, give;
Then ask if the world around you
Is better because you live.
Cho.—You are nearing the brink of Jordan,
But still there is work for you;
Then what are you going to do, brother?
Say, what are you going to do?

* One of the soul-stirring songs from the MUSICAL LEAVES, and dedicated by the Author to the Young Men's Christian Associations of the United States.

Familiar Hymns.

No. 147. *"Missionary Hymn,"* Key F.

1 ARABIA's desert ranger
  To Christ shall bow the knee,
  The Ethiopian stranger
  His glory come to see
  With off'rings of devotion,
  Ships from the isles shall meet,
  To pour the wealth of ocean
  In tribute at his feet.

2 Kings shall fall down before him,
  And gold and incense bring;
  All nations shall adore him—
  His praise all people sing;
  For he shall have dominion
  O'er river, sea, and shore,
  Far as the eagle's pinion
  Or dove's light wing can soar.

3 O'er every foe victorious,
  He on his throne shall rest;
  From age to age more glorious,
  All blessing and all blest.
  The tide of time shall never
  His covenant remove;
  His name shall stand forever—
  His great, best name of Love.

No. 148. *" Zion,"* Key D.

1 FATHER, let thy benediction,
  Gently falling as the dew,
  And thy ever-gracious presence,
  Bless us all our journey through,
  May we ever
  Keep the end of life in view!

2 Young in years, we need the wisdom
  Which can only come from thee;
  In the morn of our existence
  Let us thy salvation see,
  Changed in spirit.
  Then shall we thy children be.

3 When temptation shall assail us,
  When we falter by the way,
  Let thine arm of strength defend us,
  Saviour, hear us when we pray.
  Thou art mighty,
  Be thou then our rock and stay.

4 Praise and blessing, power and glory,
  Will we render, Lord, to thee;
  For the news of thy salvation
  Shall extend from sea to sea.
  All the nations
  Joyfully shall worship thee.

No. 149. *" Martyn,"* Key F.

1 HARK! what cry arrests my ear!
  Hark! what accents of despair!
  'Tis the heathen's dying prayer,
  Friends of Jesus, hear, O hear!
  " Men of God, to you we cry,
  Rests on you our tearful eye;
  Help us, Christians, or we die!
    Die in dark despair, despair!"

3 Hasten, Christians, haste to save;
  O'er the land and o'er the wave,
  Dangers, death, and distance brave.
  Hark! for help they call, t ey call
  Afric bends her suppliant knee—
  Asia spreads her hands to thee:
  Hark! they urge the heaven-born plea,
  " Jesus died for me, for me."

3 Haste, then, spread the Saviour's name;
  Snatch the firebrands from the flame;
  Deck his glorious diadem
  With the ransomed souls of men.
  See! the pagan altars fall!
  See! the Saviour reigns o'er all!
  Crown him, crown him Lord of all!
  Echoes round the poles, the poles.

No. 150. *" Greenville,"* Key F.

1 JESUS yet shall reign victorious,
    All the earth shall own his sway!
  He will make his kingdom glorious—
    He shall reign through endless day.
  See the ancient idols falling,
    Worshipp'd once, but now abhorr'd!
  Men on Jesus now are calling,
    Zion's King, by all adored.

No. 151. *" Webb,"* Key Bb.

1 To Thee, O blessed Saviour,
    Our grateful songs we raise;
  Oh tune our hearts and voices
    Thy holy name to praise.
  'Tis by thy sovereign mercy
    We're here allowed to meet,
  To join with friends and teachers
    Thy blessing to entreat.

2 Oh, may thy precious gospel
    Be publish'd all abroad
  Till the benighted heathen
    Shall know and serve the Lord
  Till o'er the wide creation
    The rays of truth shall shine,
  And nations now in darkness
    Arise to light divine.

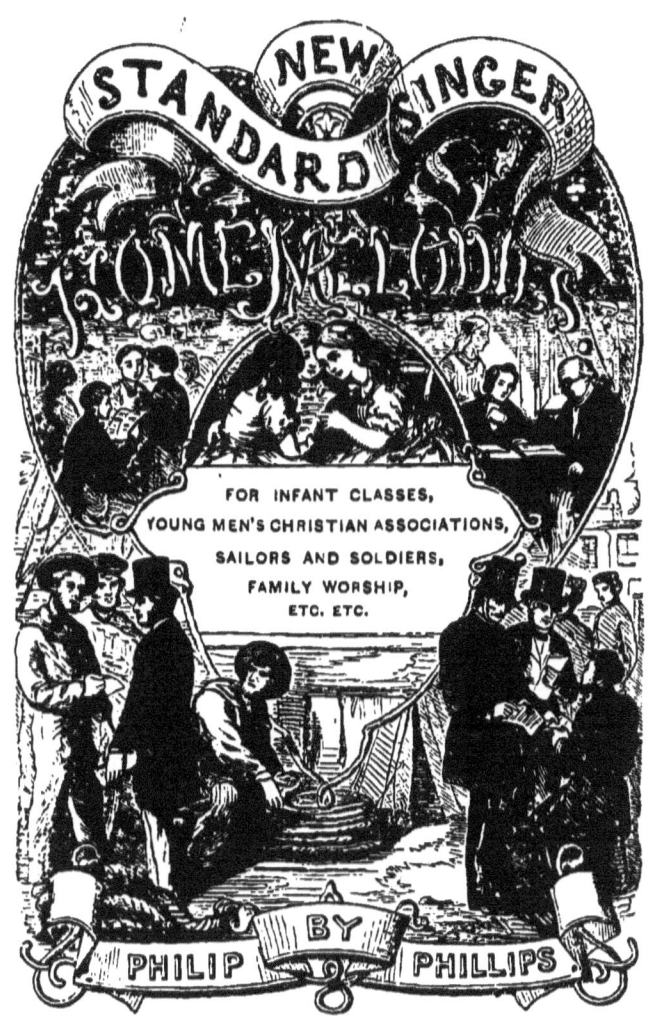

NEW STANDARD SINGER

HOME MELODIES

FOR INFANT CLASSES,
YOUNG MEN'S CHRISTIAN ASSOCIATIONS,
SAILORS AND SOLDIERS,
FAMILY WORSHIP,
ETC. ETC.

BY PHILIP PHILLIPS

PHILIP PHILLIPS, Author and Publisher,
805 Broadway, New York.
HITCHCOCK & WALDEN,
Cincinnati, Chicago, and St. Louis.

The Love of God.

No. 152

Arr. by Philip Phillips.

Scholars.

" O that men would praise the Lord for his goodness."

1. What led the Son of God To leave his throne on high,
2. What moves him to im - part His spi - rit from a - bove,

To shed his pre - cious blood; To suf - fer and to die?
There-by to fill our hearts With heaven - ly peace and love?

Teachers.

His pure and bound - less love to us Led him to die and
His pure and bound - less love to us Moves him to give his

suf - fer thus, . Led him to die and suf - fer thus.
Spi - rit thus, . Moves him to give his Spi - rit thus.

Scholars.

3 Why are we taught to pray,
  And read His word of truth,
  To keep His holy day,
  And serve Him in our youth?

Teachers.

His pure and boundless love to us
Has raised up friends to teach us thus.

Scholars.

4 Our warmest thanks we owe,
  To Thee, O God of grace!
  Our hearts should overflow
  In grateful love and praise;

Teachers.

Help us, O Lord, to praise Thee thus,
For Thine amazing love to us.

Who is He in Yonder Stall.*

No. 153

B. R. HANBY.

" Though he was rich, yet for our sakes he became poor."

1. " Who is He   in yon - der stall,   At whose feet   the shepherds fall !"
2. " Who is He   in yon - der cot,   Bending to   his toilsome lot !"

CHORUS.

'Tis   the Lord— oh, wondrous sto - ry !— 'Tis the Lord,   the King of

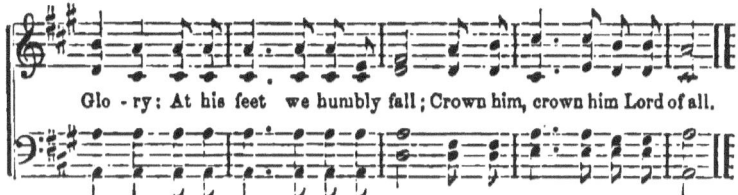

Glo - ry ; At his feet   we humbly fall ; Crown him, crown him Lord of all.

3. " Who is He who stands and weeps
    At the grave where Lazarus sleeps !"
    Cho.—'Tis the Lord, etc.

4. " Who is He, in deep distress,
    Fasting in the wilderness !"
    Cho.—'Tis the Lord, etc.

5. " Lo ! at midnight, who is He
    Prays in dark Gethsemane !"
    Cho.—'Tis the Lord, etc.

6. " Who is He, in Calvary's throes,
    Asks for blessings on his foes !"
    Cho.—'Tis the Lord. etc.

7. " Who is He that from the grave
    Comes to heal, and help, and save !"
    Cho.—'Tis the Lord, etc.

8. " Who is He that on yon throne
    Rules the world of light alone !"
    Cho.—'Tis the Lord, etc.

* From "CHAPEL GEMS," by permission.

No. 154 · **Eternal Joys.** Dr. Thos. Hastings.

"He that overcometh shall inherit all things; and I will be his God, and he shall be my son."

Children. Tell us now, the joys of heaven, Ye who know a Saviour's love; What to Christians will be giv - en, In that glorious world a - bove?

CHORUS TO BE SUNG BY THE TEACHERS.

Human tongue can ne'er declare, All that they inherit there, All that they inherit there.

Human tongue can ne'er declare, All that they inherit there, All that they inherit there.

Children.

2 Will they dwell with Christ for ever,
In the realms beyond the tomb?
And will he be absent never,
From the christian's final home?

Teachers.

They with Christ shall ever dwell,
See his face, his wonders tell.

Children.

3 Will they see the Father's glory,
And the Holy Spirit's grace,
While they sing redemption's story
In that holy happy place?

Teachers.

They shall see that vision blest,
When they enter into rest.

Children.

4 Lead us then to that salvation,
Where the living waters flow,
Guide us to that heavenly station,
For the way full well ye know.

Teachers.

All these blessings they receive,
Who in Jesus Christ believe.

Be a Lover of the Lord.

No. 155

S. J. VAIL.

"I have loved thee."

1. Am I a sol-dier of the cross,—A foll'wer of the Lamb,—And shall I
2. Must I be car-ried to the skies On flowery beds of ease; While others

CHORUS.

fear to own his cause Or blush to speak his name? You must be a lov-er of the
fought to win the prize, And sail'd through bloody seas? You must be, &c.

Lord, You must be a lov - er of the Lord, Yes, you must be a

lov - er of the Lord, If you would go to heav'n, If you would go to heav'n.

3.

Are there no foes for me to face?
Must I not stem the flood?
Is this vile world a friend to grace,
To help me on to God?—*Cho.*

4.

Since I must fight if I would reign,
Increase my courage, Lord;
I'll bear the toil, endure the pain,
Supported by thy word.—*Cho.*

No. 156   **My Home is There.***   Wm. B. Bradbury.

"In my Father's house are many mansions."

1. A - bove the waves of earth - ly strife, A - bove the

ills and cares of life. Where all is peace - ful, bright, and

fair; My home is there, My home is there.

CHORUS.

My beau - ti - ful home,............ My beau - ti - ful

My beau - ti - ful home,...... My

home,... .... In the land where the glo - ri - fied

beau - ti - ful home,

From Fresh Laurels by permission of Biglow & Main

* This is one of the beautiful songs, sung by the children at the church in Mont Clair, on the funeral occasion of Wm. B. Bradbury.

ev - er shall roam, Where an - gels bright..... wear crowns of

Where an - gels, an - gels bright, wear crowns, wear

light,........ My home is there, my home is there.

crowns of light,

2.

Where living fountains sweetly flow,
Where buds and flowers immortal grow,
Where trees their fruits celestial bear ;
My home is there, my home is there.
Cho.—My beautiful home, my beautiful home,
In the land where the glorified ever shall roam,
Where angels bright wear crowns of light,
My home is there, my home is there.

3.

Away from sorrow. doubt and pain,
Away from worldly loss and gain,
From all temptation, tears and care ;
My home is there, my home is there.
Cho.—My beautiful home, my beautiful home,
In the land where the glorified ever shall roam,
Where angels bright wear crowns of light,
My home is there, my home is there.

4.

Beyond the bright and pearly gates,
Where Jesus, loving Saviour, waits,
Where all is peaceful, bright, and fair ;
My home is there, my home is there.
Cho.—My beautiful home, my beautiful home,
In the land where the glorified ever shall roam,
Where angels bright wear crowns of light,
My home is there, my home is there.

True Worship.

No. 157   DR. THOS. HASTINGS.

" The Lord shall ye fear, and him shall ye worship."

1. Chil - dren, when we sing of Je - sus, Oh, re - mem - ber that, he sees us, That he looks in - to the heart: Do you love him while you fear him? Do you trust him, and draw near him? Do not act the tri - fler's part.

2. Je - sus, once for sin - ners bleed - ing, Now in heaven is in - ter - ced - ing, Let us seek to be for - giv'n, Let us feel that sin is hate - ful, Let us all be ve - ry grate - ful, While we lift our songs to heaven.

3 When for prayer we've met together,
Do you tell our heavenly Father
Of the very things you need?
Do you ask, when we are praying?
Do you feel what we are saying—
Are you giving earnest heed?

4 Let us not be present merely,
Let us worship God sincerely,
When we sing, and when we pray:
When we're reading, when we're speaking,
When his blessing we are seeking.
Let our thoughts ne'er go astray.

At Jesus' Feet. C. M.

No. 158

Dr. Thos. Hastings.

"And all things whatsoever ye shall ask in prayer, believing, ye shall receive."

Quick but Gentle.

1. A lit - tle child at Je - sus' feet, His blessings I would
2. How kind and gra - cious he appears, How full of ten - der

share; He sits up - on the mer - cy - seat, To
love; Quick to re - lieve from all my fears, And

heark - en un - to prayer, To heark - en un - to prayer.
bid me look a - bove, And bid me look a - bove,

3 Not every ardent wish is met,
  Nor all I ask bestowed,
But I would never once forget
  That wisdom dwells with God.

4 Where he withholds, full well he knows,
  'Tis better than to give;

And when he graciously bestows,
  I joyfully receive.

5 I would be ever satisfied,
  In waiting his behest;
No real want will be denied,
  He giveth what is best.

Jesus, Saviour, Pity Me.

No. 159

" The Lord pitieth them that fear him. "

1. Je - sus, Sa-viour, pi - ty me! Hear me when I cry to thee!

I've   a ve - ry sin - ful heart, Full of sin in ev' - ry part.

I can ne - ver make it good: Wilt thou wash me   in thy blood ?

Je - sus, Sa-viour, pi - ty   me ! Hear me when I   cry to thee!

2 Short has been my pilgrim way,
　Yet I'm sinning ev'ry day;
　Though I am so young and weak,
　Lately taught to run and speak—

Yet in evil I am strong,
Far from thee I've lived too long ;
Jesus, Saviour, pity me !
Hear me when I cry to thee !

No. 160 ## The Angel Band.* <small>JOHN MARCH, Jun.</small>

"And God shall wipe away all tears from their eyes, and there shall be no more death."

1. Go, o - pen wide the door, mo-ther, And let the an - gels in; They are so bright and fair, mother, So pure and free from sin. I hear them speak my name, mother; They soft - ly whisper, "Come!" O, let the an - gels in, mother, They've come to take me home.

2 I know that death has come, mother,
His hand is on my brow ;
You cannot keep me here, mother—
For I must leave you now.
The room is growing dark, mother—
I thought I heard you weep ;
'Tis very sweet to die mother,
Like sinking into sleep!

3 I now must say farewell, mother,
For I am going home !
Now open wide the door, mother,
And let the angels come !
And let them bear me far away,
Up to the world of love,
The city where the angels stay,
The brighter world above.

* A litt e girl, who was about to expire, said to her mother, "Now, mother, I'm dying. Open
the door and let the angels in—they've come to take me home." Better be sung as a solo.

Children's Promise.

No. 161

W. Hixom.

"Of such is the Kingdom of Heaven."

Yes, there are lit - tle ones in heav'n, Babes such as we a - round the throne, To whom the King of kings hath given A glo - ry like his own. Je - sus, thy mer - cy, rich and free, Hath suf - fered them to come to thee!

2 O let us think of them to day—
Their sweet and everlasting song,
And hope to sing as loud as they
In the same heaven ere long.
Jesus! may this our portion be—
O suffer us to come to thee!

3 To come with humbleness of mind,
With simple faith and earnest prayer,
To seek thy precious cross, and find

Peace—joy—salvation there.
O set our sin-bound spirits free,
And suffer us to come to thee!

4 To come while we are young and gay,
While life, and joy, and hope run high,
To come in sorrow's gloomiest day,
'To come when death is nigh.
Lord, in that day our guardian be,
And suffer us to come to thee.

He'll Carry us Through.*

No. 162.

" Looking unto Jesus, the author and finisher of our faith."

1. Yield not to tempta - tion, For weakness is sin; Each vict'ry will
2. Shun e- vil compan - ions, Bad language dis - dain, God's name hold in
3. To him that o'ercom - eth God giveth a crown; Thro' faith we shall

help us Some other to win; Fight manful-ly onward, Dark passions sub-
rev'rence, Nor take it in vain; Be thoughtful and earnest, Kind-hearted and
conquer, Tho' oft-en cast down; He who is our Saviour Our strength will re-

- due, Look ev - er to Je - sus, He'll car - ry you through.
true, Look ev - er, etc.
new, Look ev - er, etc.

Refrain.

Ask the Sav- iour to help you, Comfort, strengthen and keep you,

Repeat pp, ad lib.

He is will- ing to aid you, He will car - ry you through.

* From "Palmer's Sunday School Music," by permission.

8

The Good Shepherd.

No. 163   Dr. Thos. Hastings.

" He shall gather the lambs with his arm, and carry them in his bosom."

Quick, but Gentle.

1. Shep-herd, while thy flock are feed-ing, Take these

lambs In thine arms, For heaven's nur - ture plead-ing.

2. With thy chosen ones connected,
   Oft they run,
   Wand'ring on,
By the flock neglected.

3. Shepherd, every grace combining,
   Keep these lambs
   In thine arms,
On thy breast reclining.

O, How I Love Jesus!

(May be sung after any tune, where thought proper.)

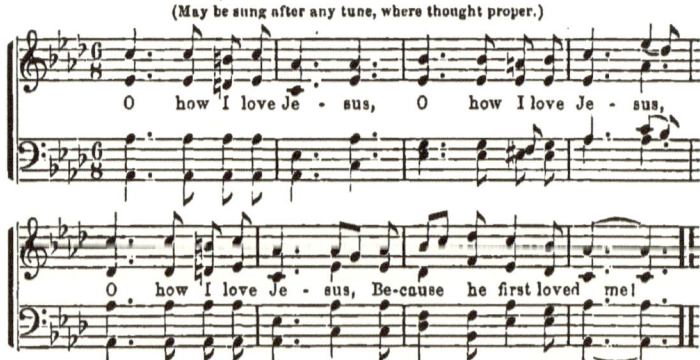

O how I love Je - sus, O how I love Je - sus,

O how I love Je - sus, Be-cause he first loved me!

" God hath chosen the weak things of the world, to confound the things that are mighty."

1. God intrusts to all, Talents few or many; None so young and small, That they have not any.

Tho' the great and wise, Have a greater number, Yet my one I prize, And it must not slumber.

2 Every little mite,
  Every little measure,
Helps to spread the light,
  Helps to swell the treasure.
Little drops of rain
  Bring the springing flowers;
And I may attain
  Much by little powers.

3 God intrusts to all,
  Talents few or many ;
None so young and small,
  That they have not any.
God will surely ask,
  Ere I enter heaven,
Have I done the task
  Which to me was given "

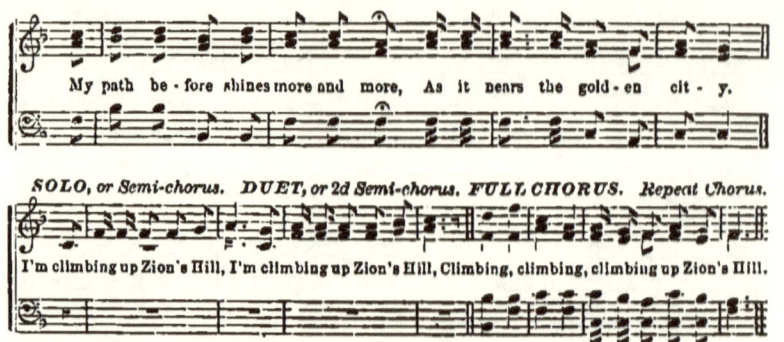

My path be - fore shines more and more, As it nears the gold - en cit - y.

SOLO, *or Semi-chorus.* DUET, *or 2d Semi-chorus.* FULL CHORUS. *Repeat Chorus.*

I'm climbing up Zion's Hill, I'm climbing up Zion's Hill, Climbing, climbing, climbing up Zion's Hill.

2 I know I'm but a little child,
  My strength will not protect me;
But then I am the Saviour's lamb,
  And he will not neglect me.
Then all the time I'll try to climb
  This holy hill of Zion,
For I am sure the way is pure,
  And on it comes " no lion."—*Cho.*

3 Then come with me, we'll upward go,
  And climb this hill together;
And as we walk we'll sweetly talk,
  And sing as we go thither.
Then mount up still God's holy hill,
  Till we reach the pearly portals,
Where raptured tongues proclaim the songs
  Of the shining-robed immortals.—*Cho.*

Pilgrim on the Road.*

No. 168.

Jas. M. North.

"For we seek a city which hath foundations."

1. I'm a pilgrim, pilgrim on the road, Lit-tle pilgrim on the road To the
2. I was burden'd, burden'd with a load, Heavy burden'd with a load When I
3. I was wea-ry, wea-ry of the load, Ver-y wea-ry of the load, As I

cit-y of our God; I have left the way of sin That I had long wander'd
started on the road: 'Twas the sin that I had done; My own hand had laid it
totter'd o'er the road; But the Saviour took the pack From the lit-tle pilgrim's

Refrain.

in, And I'm pressing tow'rd the land, the land of glory.   On, on, on! I'm trav'ling
on Ere I started for the land, the land of glo-ry,   On, on, &c.
back, And I'm trav'ling on with lightsome heart to glory.   On, on, &c.

on! On to glo-ry! on to glo-ry! I have left the way of sin That I

long have wander'd in, And I'm trav'ling to the land, the land of glo-ry.

* Words by Rev. H. O. M'Cook, by permission.

The Pilot.

No. 169

"The Lord shall guide thee continually."

1. Toss'd up - on life's rag - ing bil - low, Sweet it is, O
Thou the faith - ful watch art keep - ing, "All, all's well," thy

Lord, to know,
con - stant cheer. } Thou did'st press a sail - or's pil - low,

And canst feel a sail - or's woe. Ne - ver slumb'ring

ne - ver sleep - ing, Though the night be dark and drear.

2.

And though loud the wind is howling,
  Fierce though flash the lightning's red:
Darkly though the storm-cloud's scowling
  O'er the sailor's anxious head;
Thou canst calm the raging ocean,
  All its noise and tumult still,
Hush the tempest's wild commotion,
  At the bidding of thy will.

3.

Thus my heart the hope will cherish,
  While to thee I lift mine eye,
Thou wilt save me ere I perish,
  Thou wilt hear the sailor's cry.
And though mast and sail be riven,
  Life's short voyage will soon be o'er;
Safely moored in heaven's wide haven,
  Storm and tempest vex no more.

None but Jesus.*

No. 170   Rev. R. Lowry.

"How shall we escape if we neglect so great salvation."

1. Weep - ing will not save me— Tho' my face were bathed in tears,
2. Work - ing will not save me— Pur - est deeds that I can do,

That could not al - lay my fears Could not wash the sins of years—
Ho - liest thought and feel-ings too, Can - not form my soul a - new—

CHORUS.

Weep-ing will not save me. Jesus wept and died for me; Je-sus suffered
Work-ing will not save me. Jesus wept, &c.

on the tree; Je - sus waits to make me free; He a-lone can save me.

3 Waiting will not save me—
Helpless, guilty, lost, I lie;
In my ear is mercy's cry;
If I wait I can but die—
   Waiting will not save me.
   Cho.—Jesus wept, &c.

4 Faith in Christ will save me—
Let me trust thy weeping Son,
Trust the work that he has done;
To his arms, Lord, help me run—
   Faith in Christ will save me.
   Cho.—Jesus wept, &c.

* By permission.

No. 171   **How Shall I Die.**   PHILIP PHILLIPS.

" Prepare to meet thy God."

1. When, where, and how shall I die? In

youth or in manhood, or when I shall stand O'er-mantled with age, with my

staff in my hand? At morn, or at midnight, or when shall it be, Thou

spir - it of truth, dare I hear it from thee? When, where, and how shall I die?

CHORUS or QUARTETTE.

My bless - ed Re - deem - er, my Sav - iour, my all, Pre - pare me for death, Ere thy summons shall call.

2.

When, where, and how shall I die?
Will strangers attend me, or kindred be near,
And voices that love me fall sweet on my ear?
Or shall I alone through the valley depart
With none to support me or comfort my heart?
When, where, and how shall I die?
Cho.—When o'er the dark river I pass from the shore,
　　Go with me, dear Jesus,
　　I ask for no more.

3.

When, where, and how shall I die?
By illness protracted, or hasty decline,
Will pain, or a tranquil departure be mine?
Will reason forsake me or conscience be clear,
Will hope or its angel of mercy be near?
When, where, and how shall I die?
Cho.—Oh, grant I may pillow my head on thy breast,
　　Thou guide of the faithful,
　　And God of the blest.

4.

When, where, and how shall I die?
Though solemn the question, the time, or the place,
'Twill matter but little if God, by his grace,
Will help me to labor, to watch, and to pray,
And wait for his coming; I know not the day,
When, where, and how I shall die.
Cho.—One blessing I crave, 'tis the greatest of all,
　　Prepare me for death
　　Ere thy summons shall call.

Guide. 7s.

No. 172.

M. M. WELLS.

"He will guide us into all truth."

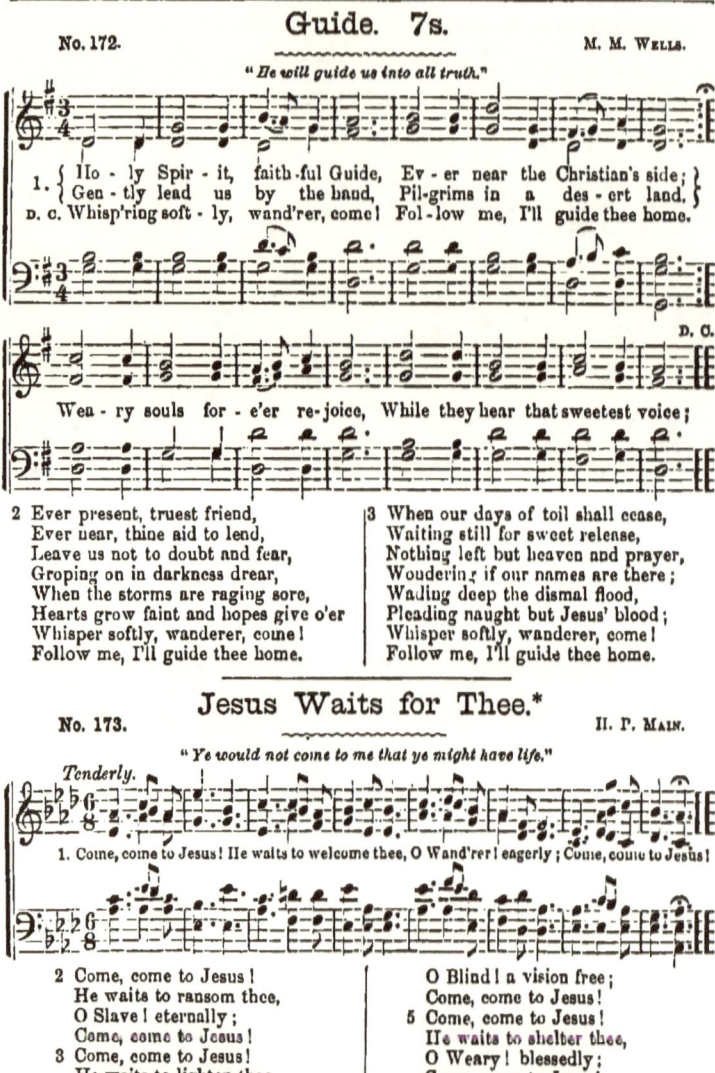

1. { Ho - ly Spir - it, faith - ful Guide, Ev - er near the Christian's side; }
{ Gen - tly lead us by the hand, Pil-grims in a des - ert land. }
D. C. Whisp'ring soft - ly, wand'rer, come! Fol - low me, I'll guide thee home.

D. C.

Wea - ry souls for - e'er re- joice, While they hear that sweetest voice;

2 Ever present, truest friend,
Ever near, thine aid to lend,
Leave us not to doubt and fear,
Groping on in darkness drear,
When the storms are raging sore,
Hearts grow faint and hopes give o'er
Whisper softly, wanderer, come!
Follow me, I'll guide thee home.

3 When our days of toil shall cease,
Waiting still for sweet release,
Nothing left but heaven and prayer,
Wondering if our names are there;
Wading deep the dismal flood,
Pleading naught but Jesus' blood;
Whisper softly, wanderer, come!
Follow me, I'll guide thee home.

Jesus Waits for Thee.*

No. 173.

H. P. MAIN.

"Ye would not come to me that ye might have life."

Tenderly.

1. Come, come to Jesus! He waits to welcome thee, O Wand'rer! eagerly; Come, come to Jesus!

2 Come, come to Jesus!
He waits to ransom thee,
O Slave! eternally;
Come, come to Jesus!
3 Come, come to Jesus!
He waits to lighten thee,
O Burdened! graciously;
Come, come to Jesus!
4 Come, come to Jesus!
He waits to give to thee,

O Blind! a vision free;
Come, come to Jesus!
5 Come, come to Jesus!
He waits to shelter thee,
O Weary! blessedly;
Come, come to Jesus!
6 Come, come to Jesus!
He waits to carry thee,
O Lamb! so lovingly;
Come, come to Jesus!

* From "HALLOWED SONGS"

"Keep on Praying."*

No. 174.

T. E. PERKINS.

"Pray without ceasing."

1. { Long my spi - rit pined in sor-row, Watching, waiting all in vain;
   { Wait - ing for a gold-en morrow, (OMIT..

Free from earthly care and pain. When I heard a sweet voice saying, In the accents

of a friend, Cheer up, brother, "keep on praying," Keep on praying to the end.

Chorus.

When our wayward thoughts are straying, When God's mercy seems delaying,

Then in faith we'll keep on praying, Keep on praying, Keep on praying to the end.

2 Ye, who sigh for holy pleasures,
　Ye, who mourn your load of sin,
　"Keep on praying," heavenly treasures,
　In the end you're sure to win.
　Wrestle with the Lord of glory,
　Lay your troubles at his feet,
　Plead with faith in Calvary's story
　Till your joys are all complete.
　　When our, etc.

3 How the angel band rejoices,
　When a kneeling mortal prays;
　Hear them cry in heavenly voices,
　"Keep on praying," all your days.
　Pray until you reach fair Canaan,
　Reach the pearly gates of day,
　Then your bliss shall end in glory,
　And shall never pass away.
　　When our, etc.

* From "SABBATH CAROLS," by permission.

Battling for the Lord. T. E. Perkins.

"I must work the works of him that sent me while it is day; the night cometh when no man can work."

1. We've list-ed in a ho-ly war, Battling for the Lord! E - ter-nal life, e -

ter-nal joy, Battling for the Lord! We'll work till Je-sus comes, We'll

work till Jesus comes, We'll work till Jesus comes, And then we'll rest at home.

2 Under our captain Jesus Christ,
  Battling for the Lord !
We've listed for this mortal life,
  Battling for the Lord !
  We'll work, etc.

3 We'll fight against the powers of sin,
  Battling for the Lord !
In favour of our heavenly King,
  Battling for the Lord !
  We'll work, etc.

4 And when our warfare here is o'er,
  Battling for the Lord !
This strife we'll leave, and war no more,
  Battling for the Lord !
  We'll work, etc.

5 Our friends and kindred there we'll meet,
  On the heavenly shore !
And ground our arms at Jesus' feet,
  On the heavenly shore !
  We'll work, etc.

CODA, FOR THE LAST VERSE.

Home, home, sweet, sweet home! Prepare me, dear Saviour, for glory, my home.

Not with the Multitude.*

No. 176   Rev. R. Lowry.

"And seeing the multitude he went up into the mountain to pray."

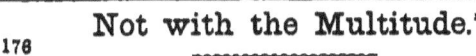

1. { It is not with the mul - ti - tude, I feel my heart re - vive;
   { It is not with the gid - dy throng, My soul is kept a - live;

'Tis in the si - lent sa cred hour, When none but God is near,

My heart is fill'd with sa - cred love, And rev - e - ren - tial fear,

CHORUS.

Not with the mul - ti - tude, Not with the mul - ti - tude, No

place is so sweet as the mer - cy - seat, When none but God is near.

2 It is not with the multitude,
  I hear the still, small voice,
Which whispers messages of love,
  And bids my heart rejoice;
Oh, no; 'tis when withdrawn from earth,
  And every earth-bound tie,
I heard thy kind parental voice,
  And "Abba, Father," cry.—*Cho.*

3 It is not with the multitude,
  My sweetest joys arise;
Nor even with the saints on earth,
  Though bound by sacred ties;
The fellowship of saints is sweet,
  But sweeter, better far,
Is fellowship with Christ my Lord,
  The bright and Morning Star.—*Cho.*

* By permission.

Familiar Hymns.

No. 177.   Key E.
1 I HAVE a Father in the promised land,
   I have a Father in the promised land.
   My Father calls me; I must go,
   To meet him in the promised land.
   I'll away, I'll away to the promised
       land;
   My Father calls me; I must go,
   To meet him in the promised land.

2 I have a Saviour in the promised land;
   I have a Saviour in the promised land.
   My Saviour calls me; I must go,
   To meet him in the promised land.
   I'll away, I'll away to the promised
       land!
   My Saviour calls me; I must go,
   To meet him in the promised land.

4 I hope to meet you in the promised land,
   I hope to meet you in the promised land.
   At Jesus' feet a joyous band,
   We'll praise him in the promised land.
   We'll away, we'll away to the prom-
       ised land!
   At Jesus' feet a joyous band,
   We'll praise him in the promised land

No. 178.   Key G.
1 Oh, do not be discouraged,
   For Jesus is your friend!
   Oh, do not be discouraged,
   For Jesus is your friend!
   He will give you grace to conquer,
   He will give you grace to conquer,
   And keep you to the end.

   CHORUS.

   I am glad I'm in this army,
   Yes, I'm glad I'm in this army,
   Yes, I'm glad I'm in this army,
   And I'll battle for the school.

2 Fight on, ye little soldiers,
   The battle you shall win;
   Fight on, ye little soldiers,
   The battle you shall win;
   For the Saviour is your Captain,
   For the Saviour is your Captain,
   And he has vanquished sin.
   I am glad, etc.

3 And when the conflict's over,
   Before him you shall stand;
   And when the conflict's over,
   Before him you shall stand.
   You shall sing his praise forever,
   You shall sing his praise forever,
   In Canaan's happy land.
   I am glad, etc.

No. 179.   Key G.
1 AROUND the throne of God in heaven
   Thousands of children stand;
   Children whose sins are all forgiven,
   A holy, happy band;
   Singing glory, glory, glory.

2 What brought them to that world above,
   That heaven so bright and fair,
   Where all is peace, and joy, and love?
   How came those children there?
   Singing glory, glory, glory.

3 Because the Saviour shed his blood
   To wash away their sin;
   Bathed in that pure and precious blood,
   Behold them white and clean;
   Singing glory, glory, glory.

4 On earth they sought their Saviour's
       grace,
   On earth they loved his name;
   So now they see his blessed face,
   And stand before the Lamb,
   Singing glory, glory, glory.

No 180.   "*Arlington.*" Key G.
1 SEE Israel's gentle shepherd stands
   With all engaging charms;
   Hark how he calls the tender lambs,
   And folds them in his arms.

2 Permit them to approach, he cries,
   Nor scorn their humble name;
   For 'twas to bless such souls as these
   The Lord of angels came.

3 He'll lead us to the heavenly streams,
   Where living waters flow;
   And guide us to the fruitful fields
   Where trees of knowledge grow.

4 The feeblest lamb amidst the flock
   Shall be its Shepherd's care;
   While folded in the Saviour's arms,
   We're safe from every snare.

No. 181.   Key G.
1 WE are out on the ocean sailing,
   Homeward bound we sweetly glide,
   We are out on the ocean sailing
   To a home beyond the tide.
   CHO. All the storms will soon be over,
   Then we'll anchor in the harbor;
   We are out on the ocean sailing,
   To a home beyond the tide.

2 Millions now are safely landed,
   Over on the golden shore,
   Millions more are on the journey,
   Yet there's room for millions more.

3 When we all are safely anchored,[CHO.
   We will shout—our trials o'er,
   We will walk about the city,
   And we'll sing forevermore.—CHO.

NEW

STANDARD SINGER

PART V.

JOYFUL STRAINS

FOR
ANNIVERSARIES,
SUNDAY SCHOOL CONCERTS,
CELEBRATIONS,
JUBILEES, FESTIVALS, ETC.

BY
PHILIP PHILLIPS.

PHILIP PHILLIPS, Author and Publisher,
805 BROADWAY, NEW YORK.

HITCHCOCK & WALDEN,
CINCINNATI, CHICAGO, AND ST. LOUIS.

TRIUMPH OF THE CROSS.*

" God forbid that I should glory save in the cross of our Lord Jesus Christ."

Words by FANNY CROSBY.

Music by F. C. GOUGH & P. PHILLIPS.

No. 182   ## No. 1 "Prepare, O Earth."
RECIT. Bass.

Pre-pare, O earth, the way of God pre-pare, And

ff Largo.

in the des-ert let his path be straight; For, lo! the sol-i-ta-ry
lento.

p

place shall bloom, the wil-der-ness shall blos-som like the rose.

*A short oratorio for Sunday School Concerts.

No. 2. The Birth of Christ. (Angel Song.)

1. Be   not   troubled   at   my   pres-ence,   Send your
2. Go   and   bow your-selves be-fore him,   This to

i - dle   fears a - way,   Send your i - dle   fears a - way;
you shall   be the sign,   This to   you shall   be the   sign;

Lift your eyes and shout hosan-nas,   Christ the Lord is   born to - day,
Ye shall find him in   a man-ger,   In-fant Saviour,   Lord di-vine,

Christ the Lord is   born to-day.
In - fant Sav-iour, Lord divine.

No. 3. Chorus of Angels and Shepherds.

Wake, ye por - tals of the skies; An - gels, strike your

ff *CHORUS—Angels and Shepherds.*

Wake, ye por - tals of the skies; An - gels, strike your

harps a - gain: Glo - ry be to God on high, Peace on

Angels.

earth, good will to men. Hal - le - lu - jah! Hal - le - lu - jah!

Shepherds. *Angels.*

Hal - le - lu - jah! Hal - le - lu - jah! Hal - le - lu - jah!

f *Both.* ff *rall.*

Hal - le - lu - jah! Hal - le - lu - jah! A - men............

"And immediately there appeared with the angel a multitude of the heavenly hosts, praising God and saying, Glory to God in the highest, and on earth peace, good will towards men."

No. 4. Simeon and Christ in the Temple.

RECIT. Bass.

Religioso.

Lo! in the tem- ple   ag- ed Simeon stood, And when the parents brought the holy child To make him there an offering to the Lord, He took him in his trembling arms, and said, "Oh, let thy servant, Lord, depart in peace, For thy sal- vation now mine eyes have seen."

No. 5. To us a Child is born.

CHORUS.

To us a Child is born, To us a Son is given, To us a Child is

born, To us a Son is given; Thro' him the na-tions shall re - joice, And

learn the way to heaven, And learn the way to heaven; To him shall monarchs

bow, And kings be - fore him fall, The Gen - tile world his power shall

see, And own him Lord of all, And own him Lord of all.

No. 6. His Baptism.

Baptised of
His days of

John, from Jor - dan's wave, Be-hold the Sav-iour rise, And
sore temp - ta - tion past, His mis-sion now be-gan, The

see the Spir - it, like a dove, De - scend - ing
glo - rious work for which he came, To res - cue

from   the   skies, De - scend-ing from......... the skies.
fall - en _ man, To res - cue _ fall - . . en _ man.

While from a cloud that cir - cled round, Proclaimed his Fa - ther's

voice, "Lo! this is my be - lov - ed Son,

In him be-lieve, re - joice,.... In him be-lieve, re-joice."

"AND there are many things that Jesus did, which if they were written every one, I suppose that even the world itself could not contain the books that should be written."

No. 7. His Miracles.

CHORUS. *Joyfully.*

Strew the way with palm - trees, To the ho - ly cit - ty;

Children in the tem - ple Make their arch - es ring.

Strew the way with palm - trees, Shout a - loud ho - san - na,

Bow the knee be - fore him, Sa - lem's might - y King;

Bow the knee be - fore him, Sa - lem's might - y King.

SOLO.—Tenor. *Andante.*

He whose smile re-flect-ing light, Turn'd to wine the wa-ter bright;

mf

f   *p*   *legato.*

He who on the storm-y deep Hush'd the roll-ing waves to sleep;

Cleans'd the le-per by a word, Heal'd the sick, the deaf re-stored;

rit.

Repeat Chorus.

He who blest the loaves that fed Hung-ry souls with liv-ing bread,

SOLO. Bass. *Lento.*

He who touch'd the sa - ble bier, Dried the child-less wid- ow's tear,

He who then but gen - tly spoke, And her son to life a - woke,

Why re - buke the joy - ous song, Bursting from a grate-ful throng,

Rit. *Repeat Chorus.*

Cease to chide the gathering crowd, Or the stones will cry a - loud.

No. 8. His Betrayal.

p Joy hides her face, The Sav-iour is be -

trayed. By all de-serted, To the Judgment-hall is

rude - ly borne, And there condemned to die.

No. 9. Christ's Sufferings.

DUET.—Soprano and Contralto.

Surely he has borne our grief, All our sorrows he has known, He was wounded for our sins, And the winepress trod a-lone ; To the slaughter he was led, He the pure, the just, the good, Though condemned he answered not, As a lamb he meekly stood ; Tho' condemned he answered not, As a lamb he meekly stood.

lento.

f 2d Voice. *p*

p 1st Voice. *f* 2d Voice. *p* 1st Voice.

f 2d Voice. *p*

No. 10. His Crucifixion, Death and Ascension.

QUARTETT.

And now at God's right hand a - bove, He pleads our cause; O

won - drous love! Re - demp - tion's glo - rious work is done, Free

Rit. - - - - - - - *f Con spirito.*

grace to all, through Christ the Lord. Re - joice, O earth! let

heaven re - joice, And shout a - loud in cho - ral voice, Our ris - en

Rit.

Lord the tomb for-sakes, The bonds of death tri - umph- ant breaks.

10

The Story of "Christian."*

No. 183   PHILIP PHILLIPS.
Words by FANNY CROSBY.

" Thy statutes have been my songs in the house of my pilgrimage."

With care-less step he hur-ries on A-long the path of sin; The
win-dows of his soul are closed, And all is dark with-in: On
per-il's aw-ful brink he stands, A chasm yawns be-low, A
crag that scarce his feet will hold Hangs on that waste of woe.

* Theme from Bunyan's Pilgrim's Progress. A short Cantata for Sunday School Concerts, occupying fifteen minutes.

DUET.

Yet warned by conscience—see, he turns! She bids him quickly fly ; God's

Yet see, he turns! She bids him quickly fly,

Spir - it pleads with ear-nest call—Why, sin - ner, wilt thou die! Con -

demned and lost, the weight of guilt Hangs heav-y on his soul; From

Si - nai's mount its lightning's flash, And loud its thun - ders roll.

SOLO.　　　　　　　pp Echo rit.　　pp

"Where shall I go?" "I am the door," A still small voice re -

plies; He sees the cross— his bur-den falls—The Sav-iour bids him

rise ; He looks and won- ders—looks a - gain, His rap-ture, who can

speak! While from his head the springs of joy Send, wa - ter to his cheek.

CHORUS.—Soprano. *Allegro.*

And now he climbs, he climbs the toilsome hill, He nears the palace

Alto.

Tenor.

And now he climbs, he climbs the toilsome hill,

Bass.

pia.

fair,   He nears the palace fair; He views,   he   views its mountains from a-

He nears the palace fair;   He views, he views its mountains from a-

far,   And feels the ge-nial   air,   And feels the ge -nial   air;   He

far,   And feels the ge-nial   air,   And feels the ge -nial   air;   He

walks the vale and shade of death, And yet he fears no

walks the vale and shade of death, And yet he fears no

ill, And yet he fears no ill; A - pol - lyon by his

ill, And yet he fears no ill; A - pol - lyon by his

sword is crushed,Thro' God, thro' God he con-quers still, Thro'

sword is crushed,Thro' God, thro' God he con-quers still, Thro'

Faster.

God, thro' God, he con-quers still. And now be-

God, thro' God he con-quers still. And now be-

Faster.

side, be - side the tree of life, That grows in Beu-lah

side, be - side the tree of life,

land, That grows in Beulah's land, Where blooms, where blooms the

That grows in Beulah's land, Where blooms, where blooms the

gar - dens of the king, Be - hold the Pil - grim stands, Be -

gar - dens of the king, Be - hold the Pil - grim stands, Be -

Slower.

hold the Pil-grim stands: Now plunging in the dis - mal flood, Its

hold the Pil-grim stands: Now plunging in the dis - mal flood, Its

Slower.

unis.

Very slow.

wa - ters o'er him cast, Its wa - ters o'er him cast; A

wa - ters o'er him cast, Its wa - ters o'er him cast; A

Very slow.

unis.

shout! he ris - es! mounts the air! And heav'n is gained at

shout! he ris - es! mounts the air! And heav'n is gained at

last,...... A shout! he ris - es! mounts the air! And

last...... A shout! he ris - es! mounts the air! And

heav'n is gained at   last, And heav'n is gained at   last.

heav'n is gained at   last, And heav'n is gained at   last.

Part VI.] [Price 10 cents each. $8 per 100.

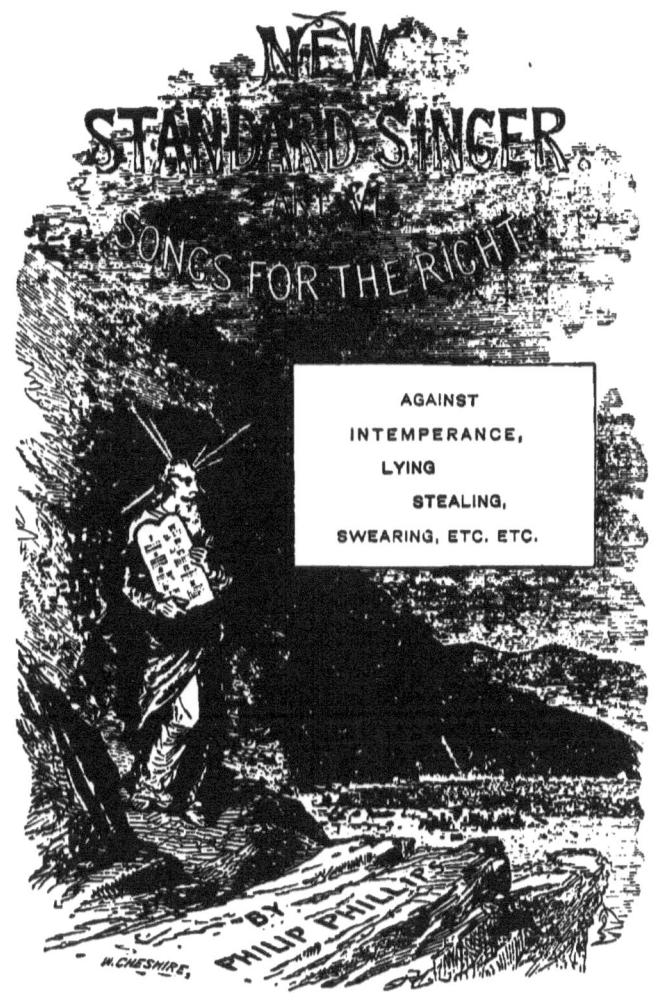

NEW

STANDARD SINGER.

SONGS FOR THE RIGHT

AGAINST

INTEMPERANCE,

LYING

STEALING,

SWEARING, ETC. ETC.

W. CHESHIRE.

BY

PHILIP PHILLIPS

PHILIP PHILLIPS, Author and Publisher,
805 BROADWAY, NEW YORK.

HITCHCOCK & WALDEN,
CINCINNATI, CHICAGO, AND ST. LOUIS.

Save the Fallen.

No. 184   S. J. VAIL.

" They have wandered as blind men in the streets ; they have polluted themselves with blood."

1. Lord, be-fore thy ho-ly al - tar, Now, thy blessing we implore,

Grant we may not faint or fal - ter 'Till our glo-rious work is o'er.

Sa-viour, help us ; we are try - ing Souls im-mor-tal to re-claim ;

Thro' intemp'rance they are dy - ing, Snatch them from its burning flame.

CHORUS.

Save the fall-en, make them so-ber ; May they feel their sins forgiv'n ;

SAVE THE FALLEN—*continued.*

When this transient life is o - ver, Give them, Lord, a place in heaven.

2.

Lo, the tempter now assailing
Hoary age and smiling youth !
Shall his cruel arts prevailing,
Stop the springs of hallowed truth ?
Lord, forbid it ! hear us pleading, —
Jesus, thou hast died to save ;
Let thy mercy interceding,
Keep them from a drunkard's grave.
Save the fallen, &c.

3.

O'er the hearts that pine with anguish,
Pour thy healing balm divine ;
O'er the wasted forms that languish,
Let the beams of comfort shine ;
In thy strength, if still united,
We the erring may restore,
Then intemp'rance, crushed and blighted,
We will banish from our shore.
Save the fallen, &c.

First Commandment with Promise.

No. 185

"Honour thy father and thy mother."

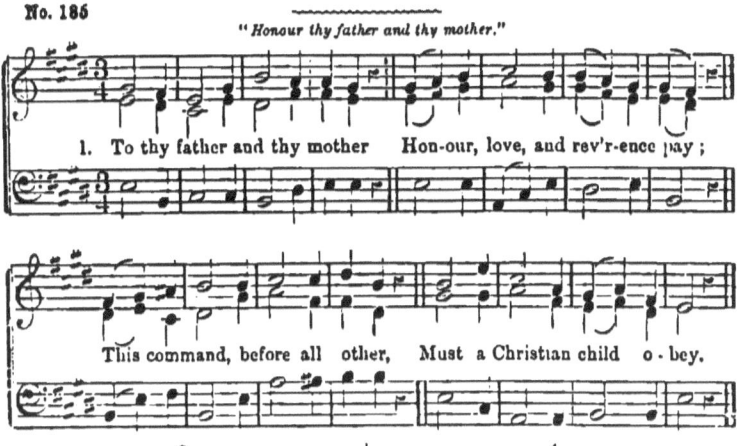

1. To thy father and thy mother   Hon-our, love, and rev'r-ence pay ;

This command, before all other,   Must a Christian child o - bey.

2.

Jesus Christ, my Lord, fulfilled it,
In his home at Nazareth,—
So his heavenly Father willed it—
While a child he dwelt beneath.

3.

Help me, Lord, in this sweet duty,
Guide me in thy steps divine ;
Show me all the joy and beauty
Of obedience such as thine.

4.

Then, when years are gath'ring o'er them,
When they're sleeping in the grave—
Sweet will seem the love I bore them,
Right the rev'rence which I gave.

5.

All my wilful ways confessing,
Now I'd keep this first command—
Seek to win the appointed blessing—
Life within the promised land.

Swear not.

No. 186   PHILIP PHILLIPS.

"But above all things swear not, but let your yea be yea, and your nay, nay."

1. They took my Sav-iour's name in vain; A thorn was in each
2. Where pleas-ure lured the soul a-way, To leave the pleas-ant

cru-el word, That pierced his sa-cred brow a-gain, While
path of truth, The cold, the heart-less, and the gay, The

Refrain.

mer-cy trem-bled as she heard. They took my Saviour's
vet-'ran sire, the care-less youth— All took my Saviour's

name in vain, And nailed him to the cross a-gain.
name in vain, And nailed him to the cross a-gain.

3.

They took my Saviour's name in vain,
  In festive hall, in crowded street;
With idle jest, and song profane,
  They trod his law beneath their feet.
They took my Saviour's name in vain,
And nailed him to the cross again.

4.

Poor, sinful man, why wilt thou spurn
  Redeeming love, so pure and free!
Awake, repent, believe, return,
  While yet his Spirit pleads for thee.
Take not my Saviour's name in vain,
Or nail him to the cross again.

No. 187   **The Morning Star.** C.M.D.   Geo. F. Root.

" We are troubled on every side, yet not distressed : we are perplexed, but not in despair."

1. Sol - dier of Christ, why thus cast down? Why drops thy nerveless hand?
Have faith and hope and courage gone? Fear'st thou the a - lien band?
Take heart, 'twill not be al-ways night: Thro' riv-en clouds a - far Gleams
down in rays of diamond light, The bright and morning star, The bright and morning star.

2 Seek not the ground in weak despair,
  Nor break 'neath suff'ring's rod ;
The fight thou wagest is the care
  Of the all-loving God.   [life;
Joy comes through sorrow; death brings
  Peace rides on battle's car ;
And beams, on darkest night of strife,
  The bright and morning star.

3 Press on the foe! God rules the years,
  Wrong shall not triumph long;
Expectant faith already hears
  Truth's glad, victorious song.

The nations soon shall own their king,
  The wise from near and far,
Once more to him their offerings bring—
  The bright and morning star.

4 Then fear not, Christian, for the right !
  Nor falter 'mid the fray ;
For truth is victor : error's night
  Flies from the coming day.
Thine eye, thro' dust and tears may see
  On heaven's broad scroll afar,
The promise sure : "I'll give to thee
  The bright and morning star."

11

The Law of God.

No. 188   Arr. by PHILIP PHILLIPS.

" Thou shalt keep therefore His statutes and His commandments."

1. God spake these words : O Israel, hear What I shall now com - mand :
Thy Lord and on - ly God am I, Who, with Al-migh-ty hand
From E-gypt's land and from the house Of bond-age set thee free ;
And there-fore, Is - rael, thou shalt have None o - ther gods but me. *Resp.*

II.	IV.
Thou shalt no graven image make,	Remember thou the Sabbath day
Nor likeness shalt thou feign,	To keep with holy care :
Of anything that heaven or earth	Six days for labour thou shalt take,
Or wa'ery deeps contain.	The seventh shalt revere.
Thou shalt not bow thyself to them,	The Lord thy God the seventh day
Nor outward worship pay ;	His Sabbath did ordain,
Much less shalt thou in heart adore,	In which thou shalt from every kind
And to an idol pray.	Of worldly work refrain.
Response—Have mercy, &c.	*Response*--Have mercy, &c.

(For Verse III. see following page.)

THE LAW OF GOD—*continued.*

III. The sa - cred name of God, thy Lord, Thou ne - ver shalt pro - fane;

For God will them not guilt-less hold Who take his name in vain. *Resp.*

(*For Verse* IV. *see preceding page.*)

V.
Thy parents honour, that thou may'st
Both long and happy live
In that bless'd land which God, thy Lord,
Did for thy dwelling give.
    Response—Have mercy, &c.

VI.
Thou shalt not kill : avoid whate'er
To life would hurtful prove ;
To all mankind thou shalt perform
The offices of love.
    Response—Have mercy, &c.

VII.
Adult'ry thou shalt not commit,
But keep thee chaste and clean :
The temples of the Lord must not
Defiled be with sin.
    Response—Have mercy, &c.

VIII.
Thou shalt not steal : detest all fraud,
And never seek by wrong
To take unto thyself what to
Another doth belong.
    Response—Have mercy, &c.

IX.
False witness thou shalt never bear
Against another's name ;
Hate lies, love truth, and e'er defend
Thy neighbour's honest fame.
    Response—Have mercy, &c.

X.
Thou shalt not covet house or wife,
Or man, or maid, of his,
Or ox, or ass, or aught whereof
He rightful owner is.
    Response—Have mercy, &c.

RESPONSE, TO BE SUNG AFTER EACH VERSE.

Have mer-cy on us, Lord, we pray, And all our hearts in - cline,

With di - li - gence and care to keep These right-eous laws of thine.

Do the Right.

Nᵒ 139   PHILIP PHILLIPS.

" No man, having put his hand to the plough, and looking back, is fit for the kingdom of God."

1. Courage, brother, do not stumble, Though thy path be dark as night;

There's a star to guide the humble; "Trust in God, and do the right."

Do the right, Do the right, "Trust in God, and do the right."

2.
Let the road be rough and dreary,
And its end far out of sight,
Foot it bravely! strong or weary,
"Trust in God, and do the right."
         Do the right, &c.

3.
Perish policy and cunning!
Perish all that fears the light!
Whether losing, whether winning,
"Trust in God, and do the right."
         Do the right, &c

4.
Trust no party, sect, or faction;
Trust no leaders in the fight:
But in ev'ry word and action,
"Trust in God, and do the right."
         Do the right, &c.

5.
Some will hate thee, some will love thee,
Some will flatter, some will slight;
Cease from man, and look above thee,
"Trust in God, and do the right."
         Do the right, &c.

No. 190   # Ten Commandments.   S. J. VAIL.

"And God spake these words, saying—"

1.   Down the ages long departed, For a moment look and wonder; Listen to the

ten commandments, Louder far than Sinai's thunder, Hear a voice which speaks to thee,

rit.   *rit.*

Thou shalt have no gods but me ; Hear a voice which speaks to thee, Thou shalt have no gods but me.

2 See the clouds are round about him,
   And the awful trumpet soundeth,
  While the Lord upon the mountain,
  His unchanging law propoundeth.
     Jealous is thy God, and thou
    To an idol shalt not bow.
          Jealous is, etc.

3 Lo ! he rides upon the tempest,
  Death and hell themselves do fear him ;
  All the worlds he hath created,
  When he speaketh, let us hear him.
    Never shalt thou take the name
    Of the Lord thy God in vain.
         Never shalt, etc.

4 Standing by the quaking mountain,
  All the hosts of Israel tremble ;
  In the presence of the holy,
  Who can trifle or dissemble?
    Thou shalt mind the Sabbath day
    Keep it holy, hear him say.
         Thou shalt, etc.

5 King of kings ! Jehovah ! Jireh !
  Thou art God, there is no other ;
  From of old we hear thee saying,

Thou shalt honour Father, Mother,
  That thy days full long may be
  In the land God gives to thee.
        That thy days, etc.

6 Awful words from Sinai sounding,
  Who shall question or gainsay them ?
  Graven deep on marble tables,
  Who shall dare to disobey them ?
    There, thou shalt not kill was writ,
    Nor adultery commit.
        There, thou shalt, etc.

7 Lo ! he looks through all disguises ;
  Tears each flimsy veil asunder ;
  Like the lightning are his glances,
  And his voice is like the thunder.
    And to us he doth reveal
    This his will, thou shalt not steal.
        And to us, etc.

8 No false witness 'gainst thy neighbour
  Shalt thou bear, and thou shalt never
  Covet aught that he possesseth,
  Saith thy God, who lives for ever ;
    The great God, who from on high
    Waits to judge thee by-and-by.
        The great God, etc.

No. 191

Depart from Me.

Theme by Miss M. Lindsay. Arr. by Philip Phillips.

"Lord, Lord, open to us. But he answered and said, Verily, I say unto you I know you not."

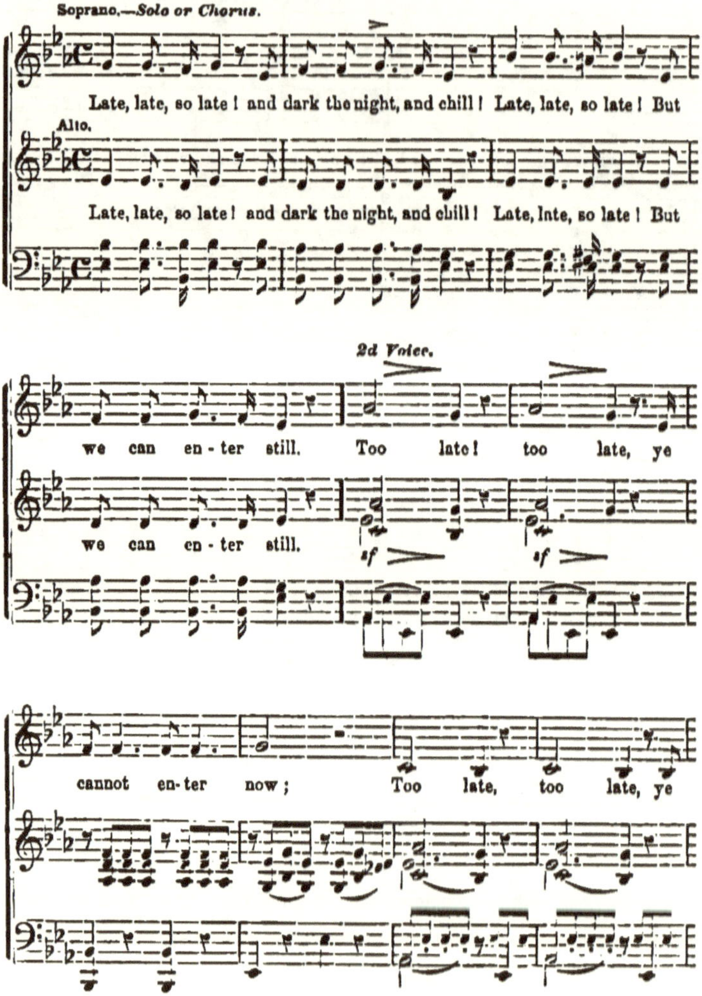
Soprano.—Solo or Chorus.
Late, late, so late! and dark the night, and chill! Late, late, so late! But
Alto.
Late, late, so late! and dark the night, and chill! Late, late, so late! But
2d Voice.
we can en - ter still. Too late! too late, ye
we can en - ter still.
sf
sf
cannot en- ter now; Too late, too late, ye

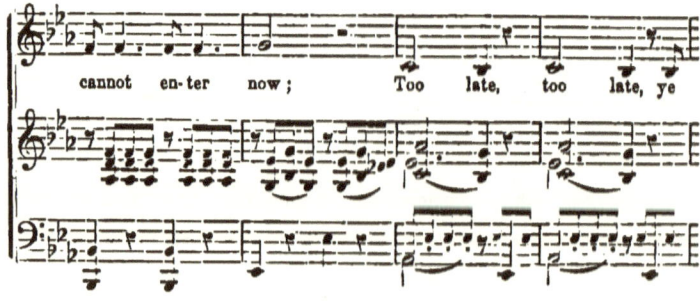

Solo or Chorus.

can - not en - ter now. No light had we: for

No light had we: for

No light had we: for

that we do repent, And learn-ing this, the Bridegroom will relent.

that we do repent, And learn-ing this, the Bridegroom will relent.

2d Voice.

Too late, too late, ye cannot en-ter now;

Too late, too late, ye cannot en-ter now.

Solo or Chorus.

No light! so late! and dark and chill the night; Oh, let us in, that

No light! so late! and dark nad chill the night; Oh, let us in, that

we may find the light, Oh, let us in, that we may find the light.

we may find the light, Oh, let us in, that we may find the light.

2d Voice.

Too   late,   too   late, ye cannot en-ter   now,

Too   late,   Too   late, ye cannot   en-ter   now.

The Fountain.

No. 192   T. C. O'KANE.

" He shall separate himself from wine and strong drink."

1. A song to the fountain! Glad-ly glow-ing, free-ly flow-ing
2. A song to the fountain! Ev-er smiling, ne'er be-guil-ing!
3. A song to the fountain! Hail the treas-ure without meas-ure!
4. A song to the fountain! Sweetly sing-ing, glad-ly spring-ing;

Down from the moun-tain, Flow-ing fresh and free!
Down from the moun-tain, Flow-ing fresh and free!
Down from the moun-tain, Flow-ing fresh and free!
Down from the moun-tain, Flow-ing fresh and free!

Chorus.

Come to the foun-tain, Come to the foun-tain,

Come to the foun-tain, Come, oh come to the
Come, oh, come to the fountain, to the foun-tain,

Come, oh, come to the fountain, Oh, come to the

Come to the foun-tain
foun-tain, to the foun-tain } Of Tem-per-ance with me.
Come to the foun-tain }

foun-tain, to the foun-tain

No. 193 ## Love not the World. H. P. Main.

"For what is a man profited if he shall gain the whole world and lose his own soul?"

1. Why should we co - vet the joy of a day— Things that will fade in a moment a - way? Toiling for wealth and its honours to gain,

CHORUS.

Why are we liv-ing for trifles so vain? Trust not the world in its beauty ar - rayed, Though at our feet all its treasures be laid; What would it profit its wealth to con - trol? What can we give in exchange for the soul?

2
We have no promise that fame will endure.
Splendour will never our pardon secure.
Gold cannot brighten the gloom of the
grave.
Only the merits of Jesus can save.
Trust not the world, etc.

3.
Blessed are they who are lowly in heart;
They, who like Mary, have chosen their
part;
Learning of Jesus, their master above,
Lessons of patience, of meekness, and love.
Trust not the world, etc.

When to say "No."

No. 194

T. MARTIN TOWNE.

"I will instruct thee and teach thee in the way which thou shalt go."

1. No is a ver-y lit-tle word; In one short breath we say it
lit-tle word,
Sometimes 'tis wrong but often right, So let me just-ly weigh it;
oft-en right,
No I must say, when asked to swear, And no when asked to gam-ble;
No, when strong drink I'm asked to share, No, to a Sunday's ram-ble.

2 No, though I'm tempted sore to lie
Or steal, and then conceal it ;
And no to sin when darkness hides,
And I alone should feel it.
Whenever sinners would entice
My feet from paths of duty,
No, I'll unhesitating cry—
No, not for price or booty.

3 God watches how this little word
By every one is spoken,
And knows those children as his own
By this one simple token.
Who promptly utters No to wrong,
Says Yes to right as surely—
That child has entered wisdom's ways
And treads her path securely.

"Renounce the Cup."

No. 195 Arr. by PHILIP PHILLIPS.

" Ye shall drink no wine, neither ye nor your sons forever."

RECITATIVE.

1. A drunkard reached his cheerless home, The storm without was dark and wild, He forced his weeping wife to roam, A wand'rer friendless with her child; As thro' the falling snow she press'd, The babe was sleeping on her breast, The babe was sleeping on her breast.

2 And colder still the winds did blow,
And darker hours of night came on,
And deeper grew the drifted snow,
Her limbs were chilled, her strength was gone.
O God I she cried in accents wild,
If I must perish, save my child ;
If I must perish, save my child.

8 She stripped the mantle from her breast,
And bared her bosom to the storm,
As round the child she wrapped the vest,
She smiled to think that it was warm.
With one cold kiss, a tear of grief,
The broken-hearted found relief,
The broken-hearted found relief.

4 At morn her cruel husband passed,
And saw her on her snowy bed,
Her tearful eyes were closed at last,
Her cheek was pale, her spirit fled ;
He raised the mantle from the child,
The babe looked up, and sweetly smiled,
The babe looked up, and sweetly smiled.

5 Shall this sad warning plead in vain [1]
Poor thoughtless one, it speaks to you ;
Now break the tempter's cruel chain,
No more your dreadful way pursue :
Renounce the cup, to Jesus fly—
Immortal soul, why will you die?
Immortal soul, why will you die?

We'll Work until we Die.

No. 196   T. MARTIN TOWNE.

" Whatsoever thy hand findeth to do do it with thy might."

1. We're looking unto Jesus, Our banner waves on high, And this our "watchword"
2. The "night of death" approaches, And angels in the sky   Re-peat the chorus

ev - er, We'll work un - til we die.   We love our Master's ser-vice, And
ev - er, Go   work un - til you die.   "Come o - ver now and help us," The

"see-ing eye to eye," With grace divine to help us, We'll work until we   die.
heathen loudly   cry, And "looking un- to   Je - sus," Go work un- til you die.

Refrain.

We'll work,   we'll work,   we'll work un-til we die, We'll work,   we'll

We'll work, we'll work un-til we die, We'll work un-til we die, We'll work, we'll work un-

work,   we'll work un - til we die.

til we die, We'll work un - til we die.

8 The field is white to harvest,
  The days are speeding by,
  Go forth, be earnest workers,
  And work until you die.
  And when the strife is over,
  Far up above the sky,
  With Jesus, blessed Jesus,
  We'll live and never die.—*Ref.*

O, Tell Me Not.

No. 197

T. C. O'KANE.

"For the drunkard and the glutton shall come to poverty."

1. O, tell me not of happiness, For me its smiles are o'er, My cup of sorrow now is full,

I shall be glad no more, I am a drunkard, old and vile, No hope is there for me.

Chorus.

Oh touch not, taste not, han-dle not, And thou shalt hap-py be,

Oh touch not, taste not, han-dle not, And thou shalt hap-py be,

2 My wife sits weeping in that home,
  Whence every joy hath fled ;
I hear her mild rebuking tone,
  O, would that I were dead !
Ah, she has died a thousand deaths,
  And shed sad tears for me.
Oh touch not, taste not, handle not,
  And she may happy be.

3 I 've children in their quiet grave,
  Some stayed behind to mourn ;
I would that they were in the land,
  Whence they could ne'er return ;
For they will rise to curse my name,
  No light, no love to see.
Oh touch not, taste not, handle not,
  And they shall happy be.

4 I 've lost my hope. I 've lost my trust,
  I 've broken every tie,
And I must wander through the world,
  A living death to die ;
My heart aches with a thousand pangs,
  Naught but despair I see.
Oh touch not, taste not, handle not,
  And thou shalt happy be.

5 We 've trod thro' many a devious path,
  Of sorrow, sin, and shame,
But there, beside the Temp'rance Pledge,
  We first restored our name.
And, brother, whosoe'er thou art,
  Stand fast, and thou shalt see
That he who tastes and handles not,
  May also happy be.

Who Hath Sorrows?

No. 198   HARVEY CAMP.

"They that tarry long at the wine."

1. Who hath sorrows? who hath woes? Who hath babblings? who hath strife?
2. Look not on the wine when red, When it foams and sparkles bright;
3. "I was stricken," thou shalt say, "Yet, when beat-en, felt no pain;

Careless wounds and fancied woes? Reddened eyes—em-bit-tered life!
Lo! it hides an ad-der's head, Like a ser-pent it will bite.
When shall wake the morning ray? I will seek it yet a-gain."

They that tar-ry at the wine; They that love the feast and song;
Wantons then will charm the eye, Things perverse thy heart disclose;
Lord, thy peo-ple's hearts in-cline To a-rouse from thoughtless ease;

Rit.

They that various drinks combine— Ear-ly haste and tar-ry long.
On the bil-lows shalt thou lie, At the mast-head seek re-pose.
Oh! as-sist the kind de-sign Of pre-vent-ing scenes like these.

Weep for the Fallen.*

No. 199 ENGLISH.

"Meekness, Temperance—Against such there is no law."

1. Weep for the fall-en! hang your heads in sor-row, And mournfully
2. Voic-es of wail-ing tell of hope-less anguish, While sorrowing

sing the requiem sad and slow. Thousands have perished by the fell destroyer;
mothers bid us onward go, Hark! to their accents, theirs the broken-hearted

Oh, weep for youth and beau-ty, Oh, weep for youth and beau-ty,
Who weep for youth and beau-ty, Who weep for youth and beau-ty,

Oh, weep for youth and beau-ty in the grave laid low!
Who weep for youth and beau-ty in the grave laid low!

3 Hear how they bid us sound the timely warning,
　While yet there is hope to shun the cup of woe.
For is it nothing, ye who see no danger,
　To weep for youth and beauty in the grave laid low?

4 Weep for the fallen; but amid your sorrow,
　Still point to the pledge that freedom can bestow,
Rescue the nation from the fell destroyer,
　For why should youth and beauty in the grave lie low?

* From "TEMPERANCE CHIMES."

12

Drinker, Turn.

No. 260   HARVEY CAMP.

" Wine is a mocker, strong drink is raging, and whosoever is deceived-thereby is not wise."

Andante.—Flowing Style.

1. Drink - er, turn and leave your bowl; Turn and

save your death - less soul; From your lips the poi - son

fling— Dash a - way th' ac-curs - ed thing.

2 Husband! turn, nor let your feet
  Enter that accursed retreat;
  Look! your partner's tearful eye
  Eloquently asks you, Why?

3 Brother! leave the place of glee;
  Quickly, quickly turn and flee!
  See your sister's swelling breast,
  Deep with anxious fear distressed.

4 Father! turn; your prattler's voice
  Bids you seek your fireside joys;
  Leave the revel; homeward haste,
  And those purer pleasures taste.

5 Fathers, brothers, husbands, come—
  Help to banish from your home,
  And from earth, the deadliest foe
  That assails our peace below.

God Speed the Right.

No. 201   FROM THE GERMAN.

"And every man that striveth for the mastery is temperate in all things."

1. Now to heaven our prayer ascending, God speed the right!
In a no - ble cause contending, God speed the right!
2 Be that prayer a - gain re - peat-ed, God speed the right!
Ne'er de - spair - ing though defeat - ed, God speed the right!

Be their zeal in heaven record - ed, With suc-cess on earth re - warded.
Like the good and great in sto - ry, If they fall, they fall with glo - ry.

God speed the right! God speed the right!

3 Patient, firm, and persevering,
  God speed the right!
Ne'er the event our danger fearing,
  God speed the right!
Pains, nor toils, nor trials heeding,
And in heaven's own time succeeding.
  God speed the right!

4 Still their onward course pursuing,
  God speed the right!
Every foe at length subduing,
  God speed the right!
Truth, thy cause, whate'er delay it,
There 's no power on earth can stay it.
  God speed the right!

Familiar Hymns.

No. 202.   *Tune,* " *Boylston,*" Key C.

1 How long, O Lord, our God,
   Shall sin and sorrow reign,
   And drunkards love to tread the road
   That leads to endless pain.

2 With zeal and pity move,
   All those that fear thy name,
   So shall they spread the cause of love
   The drunkard to reclaim.

3 Thy goodness and thy power,
   And mercy never cease;
   Thou canst the drunkard yet restore
   To happiness and peace.

4 Come, and strong drink remove,
   And bring the better day,
   When all men shall thy precepts love,
   And thy commands obey.

No. 203.   *Tune,* " *Hamburg,*" Key F.

1 Slavery and death the cup contains;
   Dash to the earth the poisoned bowl;
   Softer than silk are iron chains
   Compared with those that chafe the soul.

2 Hosannas, Lord! to thee we sing,
   Whose power the giant fiend obeys;
   What countless thousands tribute
     bring,
   For happier homes and brighter days.

3 Thou will not break the bruised reed,
   Nor leave the broken heart unbound,
   The wife regains a husband freed,
   The orphan clasps a father found.

4 Spare, Lord, the thoughtless, guide
    the blind;
   Till man no more shall deem it just,
   To live, by forging chains to bind
   His weaker brother in the dust.

No. 204.   *Tune,* " *Hebron,*" Key B♭.

1 Let temperance and her sons rejoice,
   And be their praises loud and long,
   Let every heart and every voice,
   Conspire to raise a joyful song.

2 And let the anthem rise to God,
   Whose favoring mercies so abound,
   And let his praises fly abroad,
   The circuit of the earth around.

3 His children's prayer he deigns to grant,
   He stays the progress of the foe,
   And temperance like a cherished plant,
   Beneath his fostering care shall grow.

No. 205.   *Tune,* " *Webb,*" Key B♭.

1 Lift high the temperance banner!
   Aye, proudly let it wave,
   To save the poor inebriate
   From a degraded grave.
   Then, children, at your station,
   To quell the raging storm;
   Let hearts and hands united
   Strive for a glad reform.

2 Come, join the noble army,
   Enlist now for the fight;
   Maintain our nation's honor,
   Firm stand ye for the right.
   Promote the cause of temperance,
   T' assist poor, fallen man;
   Put on the glorious armor;
   Be foremost in the van.

3 Then rally round the standard,
   And let the work go on,
   Until the last dim vestige
   Of intemperance is gone.
   Be earnest in the battle,
   Your weapons boldly wield;
   You'll surely gain the victory,
   And make the monster yield.

No. 206.   *Tune,* " *Old Hundred,*" Key G.

1 Great God, whose hand outpours the
    rills
   And springs that burst from all the hills,
   At whose command the rock was riven,
   Who send'st on all thy rain from
    heaven.

2 We bless thee for the crystal draught
   By sinless man in Eden quaffed:
   Type of that fount whose streams,
    above
   Flood endless worlds with life and love!

3 Help us to heed Thy word divine,
   And look not on the crimson wine,
   To fear and flee th' accursed thing
   As serpent's bite or adder's sting.

4 Stay thou, O Lord! the tide of death!
   Rebuke the demon's blasting breath!
   And speed, oh! speed, on every shore,
   The day when strong drink slays no
    more!

New

Standard Singer

PART-VII.

SERVICE OF SONG

FOR
SUNDAY SCHOOL CONVENTIONS,
PRAYER AND SOCIAL
MEETINGS,
DUTY OF TEACHERS,
MEETING AND PARTING.

BY·PHILIP
PHILLIPS·

PHILIP PHILLIPS, Author and Publisher,
805 Broadway, New York.

HITCHCOCK & WALDEN,
Cincinnati, Chicago, and St. Louis.

No. 207

Fear God. C.M.

R. SIMPSON.

" The fear of the Lord is the beginning of wisdom."

1. Cre - a - tor, Sov'reign Lord of all, In earth and sea and skies,

The source of wis - dom is thy fear, Oh make us tru - ly wise.

2. Teach us to know thy perfect law,
   Whose judgments truth unfold,
   More sweet than honey in the comb,
   More precious far than gold.

3. Lo! wisdom crieth at the gate,
   And spreads her hands abroad;
   O, hear the voice, ye sons of men,
   And learn the fear of God.

No. 208

Blest be the Tie. S.M.

NAGELI.

" Behold how good and how pleasant it is for brethren to dwell together in unity."

1. Blest be the tie that binds Our hearts in Christian love;

The fel - low - ship of kin - dred minds, Is like to that a - bove.

2. Before our Father's throne,
   We pour our ardent prayers,
   Our fears, our hopes, our aims are one,
   Our comforts and our cares.

3. When we asunder part,
   It gives us inward pain;
   But we shall still be joined in heart,
   And hope to meet again.

No. 209   # Rock of Ages. 7's (6 lines). Dr. T. Hastings.

"But the Lord is my defence, and my God is the rock of my refuge."

FINE.

1. Rock of A - ges! cleft for me, Let me hide my-self in Thee:
D.C. Be of sin the per-fect cure; Save me, Lord, and make me pure.

D.C.

Let the wa - ter and the blood, From thy wound-ed side which flowed,

2 Should my tears for ever flow,
Should my zeal no languor know,
This for sin could ne'er atone ;
Thou must save, and thou alone ;
In my hand no price I bring,
Simply to thy cross I cling.

3 While I draw this fleeting breath,
When mine eyelids close in death
When I rise to worlds unknown,
And behold thee on thy throne,
Rock of Ages! cleft for me,
Let me hide myself in thee.

No. 210   # Father, Take my Hand. Geo. B. Loomis.

"As for me, I will call upon God, and the Lord shall save me."

Fa - ther, I stretch my hand to thee. No other help I know ;

If thou withdraw thy - self from me, Ah! whither shall I go?

2 Surely thou canst not let me die ;
O speak, and I shall live ;
And here I will unwearied lie,
Till thou thy Spirit give.

3 How would my fainting soul rejoice,
Could I but see thy face,
Now let me hear thy quick'ning voice,
And taste thy pard'ning grace.

Realms of the Blest. 8's.

No. 211

CLEMENTS.

" It doth not yet appear what we shall be."

1. We sing of the realms of the blest, That country so bright and so fair,
And oft are its glo-ries confessed,—But what must it be to be there?
But what, But what, But what must it be to be there?
And oft are its glories confessed,—But what must it be to be there?

2.

We speak of its service of love,
Of robes which the glorified wear—
The church of the first-born above,
But what must it be to be there?

3.

Do thou, Lord, 'midst pleasure or woe,
For heaven our spirits prepare;
And shortly we also shall know,
And feel what it is to be there.

No. 212   **Welcome Home. C. M.**   Arranged.

"Come, ye blessed of my Father, inherit the kingdom prepared for you."

1. Give me the wings of faith to rise Within the veil, and see   The
2. Once they were mourners here below, And pour'd out cries and tears; They

saints a-bove, how great their joys, How bright their glories be.
wrestled hard, as we do now, With sins, and doubts, and fears.

CHORUS.

They'll sing their welcome home to me, They'll sing their welcome home to me,

1ST.   2ND.

And the angels will stand on the heavenly strand. And sing their welcome home.
D.C. And the angels will stand on the heavenly strand, And sing their welcome . . home.

D.S.

Welcome home, welcome home;

3 I ask them whence their vict'ry came:
    They, with united breath,
Ascribe their conquest to the Lamb—
    Their triumph to his death.

4 Our glorious Leader claims our praise
    For his own pattern given;
While the long cloud of witnesses
    Show the same path to heaven.

Sweet Hour of Prayer.

No. 213   WM. B. BRADBURY.*

"Evening, morning, and noon will I pray."

1. Sweet hour   of prayer! sweet hour   of prayer!   That calls   me   from   a
D. C. And oft   es-caped   the   tempter's snare   By   thy   re - turn sweet

world   of   care,   And   bids   me   at   my   Fath - er's throne Make
hour   of   prayer;   And   oft   es - caped the   tempter's snare   By

all   my wants and wish - es   known: In   sea - sons   of   dis -
thy   re - turn, sweet hour   of   prayer.

- tress   and grief, My   soul   has   oft - en   found   re - lief;

2. |: Sweet hour of prayer! :|
Thy wings shall my petition bear,
To him whose truth and faithfulness,
Engage the waiting soul to bless;
And since he bids me seek his face,
Believe his word, and trust his grace,
|: I'll cast on him my every care,
And wait for thee, sweet hour of
     prayer! :|

3. |: Sweet hour of prayer! :|
May I thy consolation share,
Till from Mount Pisgah's lofty height,
I view my home and take my flight:
This robe of flesh I'll drop, and rise
To seize the everlasting prize;
|: And shout, while passing thro' the air,
Farewell, farewell, sweet hour of
     prayer! :|

* From Fresh Laurels, by permission of BIGLOW & MAIN.

With me Abide.

No. 214

Arr. by Phillips.

"Abide with us; for it is towards evening, and the day is far spent."

1. A - bide with me; fast falls the ev - en - tide: The darkness

deep - ens; Lord, with me a - bide; When oth - er help - ers

fail, and comforts flee, Help of the helpless, oh, a - bide with me.

2 Swift to its close ebbs out life's little day;
Earth's joys grow dim, its glories pass away;
Change and decay in all around I see,
O thou who changest not—abide with me.

3 Thou on my head in early youth didst smile,
And, though rebellious and perverse meanwhile,
Thou hast not left me oft as I left thee;
On to the close, O Lord, abide with me.

4 I need thy presence every passing hour,
What but thy grace can foil the tempter's power;
Who like thyself my guide and stay can be,
Through clouds and sunshine—oh, abide with me.

5 Hold on thy cross, before my closing eyes;
Shine through the gloom, and point me to the skies;
Heaven's morning breaks, and earth's vain shadows flee,
In life and death, O Lord, abide with me.

Waiting by the River.

No. 215

Dr. Thos. Hastings.

"There shall be no more death."

1. I am wait-ing by the riv-er, And my heart has waited long; Now I
think I hear the cho-rus Of the an-gels' wel-come song; Oh, I
see the dawn is breaking On the hill-tops of the blest, "Where the
wick-ed cease from troubling, And the wea-ry be at rest."

2.

Far away beyond the shadows
  Of this weary vale of tears,
There the tide of bliss is sweeping
  Thro' the bright and changeless years;
Oh! I long to be with Jesus,
  In the mansions of the blest,
"Where the wicked cease from troubling,
  And the weary be at rest."

3.

They are launching on the river,
  From the calm and quiet shore,
And they soon will bear my spirit
  Where the weary sigh no more ;
For the tide is swiftly flowing,
  And I long to greet the blest,
"Where the wicked cease from troubling,
  And the weary be at rest."

Title Clear.

No. 216.   Freedmen's Melody arr. with Cho. by T. C. O'KANE.

" I know that my Redeemer liveth."

1. { When I can read my ti - tle clear, ti - tle clear, When I can read my ti- tle
   { I'll bid farewell to ev- ery fear, ev- ery fear, I'll bid farewell to ev-ery

clear, ti- tle clear, When I can read my ti - tle   clear, To mansions in the skies, }
fear, ev-ery fear, I'll bid farewell to every fear, And wipe my weeping eyes, }

Cho. We will stand   the   storm,   We will
We will stand, stand the storm, It will not be ver- y long; We will

an - - chor   by and   by,   by and by, We will
an - chor by   and   by, We will an - chor by   and by, We will

stand   the storm,   We will anchor by and· by.
stand, stand the storm; It will not be very long, We will anchor by and by, by and by.

2 Let cares like a wild deluge come,
  Let storms of sorrow fall—
  So I but safely reach my home,
  My God, my heaven, my all.

8 There I shall bathe my weary soul
  In seas of heavenly rest,
  And not a wave of trouble roll
  Across my peaceful breast.

Mansions Blest

No. 217   Music and Words by Dr. Thos. Hastings.

"In my Father's house are many mansions."

1. Oh,.. there are mansions blest, Tow'-ring a-bove,

Where saints de-part-ed rest In Je-sus' love;

There, there with joys un-told, His glo-ry they be-hold,

Prais-ing with harps of gold, Heaven's bliss to prove.

2 In that celestial home
  May we appear,
Where sorrows never come,
  Or guilt or fear:
Oh, what a holy place,
When all the ransomed race
Sing of redeeming grace,
  Jesus is there.

3 There, in that spirit land
  All, all is pure,
Pleasures at God's right hand,
  Ever endure.

There all in Christ complete
God's happy children meet,
Angels and friends to greet,
  Resting secure.

4 None, none can enter heaven,
  Who live in sin;
None who are unforgiven,
  Can dwell therein.
Oh! thou to Jesus fly,
His pard'ning blood is nigh,
On him alone rely,
  Wash and be clean.

Bartimeus. 8s and 7s.

No. 218

DANIEL READ.

"God forbid that I should glory, save in the cross of our Lord."

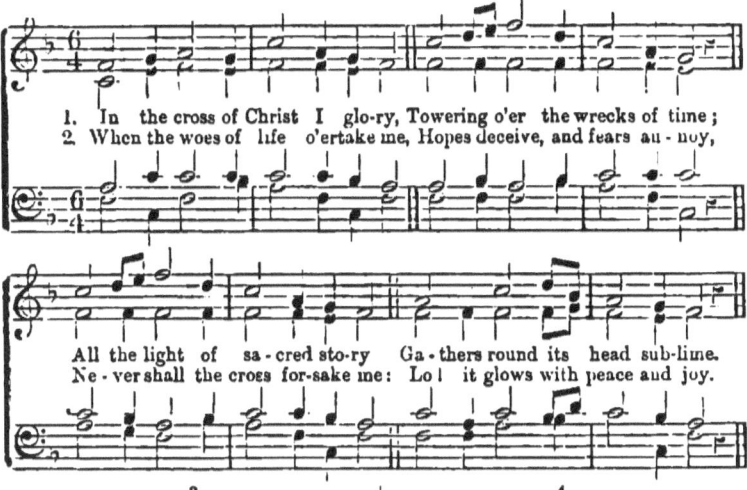

1. In the cross of Christ I glo-ry, Towering o'er the wrecks of time;
2. When the woes of life o'ertake me, Hopes deceive, and fears an - noy,

All the light of sa - cred sto-ry Ga - thers round its head sub-lime.
Ne - ver shall the cross for-sake me: Lo! it glows with peace and joy.

3.

When the sun of bliss is beaming
Light and love upon my way,
From the cross the radiance streaming,
Adds new lustre to the day.

4.

Bane and blessing, pain and pleasure,
By the cross are sanctified;
Peace is there, that knows no measure,
Joys that through all time abide.

No. 219

Bless Us To-night.

"He will bless them that fear the Lord."

1. Fa-ther of love and power, Guard thou our eve - ning hour, Shield

with thy might. For all thy care this day, Our grate-ful

BLESS US TO-NIGHT—*continued.*

thanks we pay, And to our Fa - ther pray, Bless us to-night!

2.

Jesus, Emmanuel,
Come in thy love to dwell
  In hearts contrite ;
For many sins we grieve,
But we thy grace receive,
And in thy word believe, —
  Bless us to-night.

3.

Spirit of truth and love,
Life-giving, holy dove,
  Shed forth thy light ;
Heal every sinner's smart,
Still every throbbing heart,
And thine own peace impart, —
  Bless us to-night.

No. 220   **New Haven.**   6s and 4s.

DR. THOS. HASTINGS.

"Have faith in God."

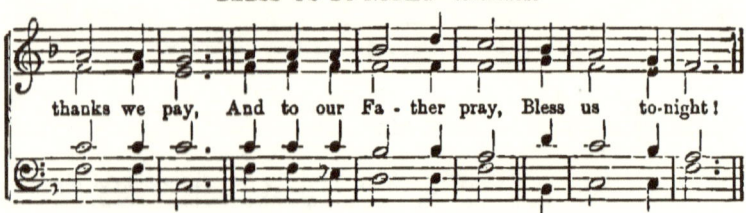

My faith looks up to thee, Thou Lamb of Cal-va-ry, Saviour di - vine! Now hear me

while I pray, Take all my guilt away, O let me from this day, Be wholly thine.

2.

May thy rich grace impart
Strength to my fainting heart ;
  My zeal inspire :
As thou hast died for me,
O may my love to thee
Pure, warm, and changeless be—
  A living fire.

3.

While life's dark maze I tread,
And griefs around me spread,
  Be thou my guide ;
Bid darkness turn to day ;
Wipe sorrow's tears away,
Nor let me ever stray
  From thee aside.

Congregational Chorus.

No. 221

PHILIP PHILLIPS.

"Let the people praise thee, O God, let all the people praise thee."

1. Yes, let our con - gre-ga-tions sing, And let our earthly temples ring With
2. O rapturous mu-sic, how sublime! I wept and thought the olden time Of

hymns of joy from ev - ery soul, In ev - ery church from pole to pole, Let
Watts' and Wesley's earnest throng Had with its flame inspired the song; O,

all u - ni - ted join, and raise This old fa - mil - iar song of praise,
let us sing with one ac - cord, Join heart and voice to praise the Lord.

CORONATION. Chorus to 1st Verse.

Firm.

1. O, for a thousand tongues to sing My great Redeemer's praise: The glories of my God and King,

The triumphs of his grace. The glories of my God and King, The triumphs of his grace.

OLD HUNDRED. Chorus to 2d Verse.

1. Praise God, from whom all blessings flow; Praise him, all creatures here below;

Praise him a - bove, ye heavenly host; Praise Father, Son, and Holy Ghost.

13

Calling us Away.

No. 222.   WALTER KITTRIDGE.

" Here we have no continuing City."

SOLO.

1. Give me the wings of faith to rise,   Within the veil, and see   The
2. Once they were mourners here be-low, And pour'd out cries and tears; They
3.   I ask them whence their vict'ry came: They, with u - nit - ed breath, As -

saints a - bove, how great their joys, How bright their glories be.
wres-tled hard, as   we   do now, With sins, and doubts, and fears.
cribe their con - quest to   the Lamb,—Their triumph to his death.

DUET.

Ma - ny   are   the friends, Who   are   wait - ing   to - day,

CHORUS to each verse.

Hap - py   on the gold - en strand;   Ma - ny ; are the voi - ces

Call-ing us   a - way, To join their glorious band; Calling us a-way,

Repeat Chorus pp

Call - ing us   a - way, Call - ing   to   the bet - ter land.

Home of the Soul.*

No. 223   Philip Phillips.

" And there shall in no wise enter into it anything that defileth, neither whatsoever worketh abomination or maketh a lie; but they which are written in the Lamb's Book of Life."

1. I will sing you a song of that beau-ti-ful land, The far a - way home of the soul, Where no storms ever beat on the glittering strand, While the years of e - ter - ni-ty roll. While the years of e - ter - ni - ty roll.

2.
O that home of the soul in my visions and dreams,
 Its bright jasper walls I can see,
Till I fancy but thinly the veil intervenes,
Between the fair city and me.
 Between the fair city, &c.

3.
There the great tree of life in its beauty doth grow,
 And the river of life floweth by :
For no death ever enters that city, you know,
And nothing that maketh a lie.
 And nothing that, &c.

4.
That unchangeable home is for you and for me,
 Where Jesus of Nazareth stands;
The king of all kingdoms forever is he,
And he holdeth our crowns in his hands.
 And he holdeth, &c.

5.
O how sweet it will be in that beautiful land,
 So free from all sorrow and pain !
With songs on our lips and with harps in our hands,
To meet one another again.
 To meet one another, &c.

" Now I saw in my Dream that these two men went in at the Gate: and lo, as they entered, they were trans-figured, and they had Raiment put on that shone like Gold. There was also that met them with Harps and Crowns, and gave them to them, the Harps to praise withal, and the Crowns in token of honor. Then I heard in my Dream that all the Bells in the City rang again for joy, and that it was said unto them, *Enter ye into the joy of your Lord.* Now just as the Gates were opened to let in the men, I looked in after them, and behold, the City shone like the Sun: the Streets also were paved with Gold, and in them walked many men, with Crowns on their heads, Palms in their hands, and golden Harps to sing praises withal. After that they shut up the Gates. Which when I had seen, I wished myself among them."

* Taken from the " Singing Pilgrim."

We'll Meet and Rest.

No. 224   PHILIP PHILLIPS.*

" There remaineth therefore a rest to the people of God."

1. Where the fa - ded flow'r shall freshen—Freshen ne - ver more to fade;
2. Where no sha - dow shall be-wil-der; Where life's vain parade is o'er;

Where the sha - ded sky shall brighten—Brighten ne - ver more to shade.
Where the sleep of sin is bro-ken, And the dream-er dreams no more;

Where the sun-blaze ne - ver scorch-es; Where the star-beams cease to chill;
Where the bond is ne - ver se-ver'd—Part-ings, clasp-ings, sob and moan—

Where no tem - pest stirs the e-choes   Of the wood, or wave, or hill;
Midnight wak - ing, twilight weeping,   Heavy noon-tide—all are done;

* These beautiful verses were handed to me by the author, Rev. H. Bonar, while at his home in
Edinburgh, Scotland.

WE'LL MEET AND REST—*continued.*

Where the morn shall wake in glad-ness, And the noon the joy pro-long;
Where the child has found its mo-ther; Where the mo-ther finds the child!

Where the day-light dies in fragrance, 'Mid the burst of ho-ly song:
Where dear fam-i-lies are gather'd, That were scatter'd on the wild:

REFRAIN.

Bro-ther, we shall meet and rest 'Mid the ho-ly and the blest!

3.	4.
Where the hidden wound is healed;	Where a blasted world shall brighten,
Where the blighted life reblooms;	Underneath a bluer sphere,
Where the smitten heart the freshness	And a softer, gentler sunshine
Of its buoyant youth resumes;	Shed its healing splendour here;
Where the love that here we lavish	Where earth's barren vales shall blossom,
On the withering leaves of time,	Putting on their robes of green,
Shall have fadeless flowers to fix on	And a purer, fairer Eden
In an ever spring-bright clime;	Be where only wastes have been;
Where we find the joy of loving,	Where a King in kingly glory,
As we never loved before—	Such as earth has never known,
Loving on, unchill'd, unhinder'd—	Shall assume the righteous sceptre,
Loving once and evermore:	Claim and wear the holy crown:
Brother, we shall meet and rest	Brother, we shall meet and rest
'Mid the holy and the blest!	'Mid the holy and the blest!

Why Not To-night? 8's.

No. 225

" Choose ye this day whom ye will serve."

PHILIP PHILLIPS.

1. Oh! do not let the word depart, And close thine eyes against the light;

Poor sinner, harden not thy heart; Thou wouldst be sav'd—why not to-night?

Why not to-night? why not to-night? Thou wouldst be sav'd—why not to-night?

2 To morrow's sun may never rise
  To bless thy long deluded sight;
  This is the time! Oh, then be wise!
  Thou would'st be saved—Why not to-night?

3 The world has nothing left to give—
  It has no new, no pure delight;
  Oh, try the life which Christians live!
  Thou would'st be saved—Why not to-night?

4 Our God in pity lingers still,
  And wilt thou thus His love requite?
  Renounce at length thy stubborn will.
  Thou would'st be saved—Why not to-night?

5 Our blessed Lord refuses none
  Who would to Him their souls unite;
  Then be the work of grace begun!
  Thou would'st be saved—Why not to-night?

Jordan's Ford.*

No. 226

REV. R. LOWRY.

" He cometh forth like a flower and is cut down."

1. Dark is many a day below, Thick the clouds that hover; Sad is many a
2. How the flitting hopes of earth, Hold us in de - ris - ion, When they draw us
3. Inward rolls the bitter surge, Drenching hearts with sorrow, Moanful flies the

bosom's throe, 'Neath its sackcloth cov - er; Wintry blasts with cruel doom,
thro' the dearth, To their false E - ly - sian! How the scenes in worldly glare,
night-ly dirge O - ver each to - mor - row; Low the plaint that sadly steals

Nip the plants we cherish, Buds of rare and sweet perfume Bloom awhile and perish.
Lure to disappoint us, Tempt our steps with visions fair, And with tears anoint us!
Over joys entombing; Drear the soul that never feels Flowers of glory blooming.

CHORUS.

But, be-yond the Jor - dan's ford, Shines the heavenly por - tal,

Where the ransomed of the Lord Pass in joys im - mor - tal.

* By permission from Chapel Melodies.

No. 227   ## St. Thomas. s.m.   WILLIAMS.

"I will praise thee, O Lord, with my whole heart."

1. A - wake and sing the   song   Of   Mo - ses and the Lamb;
2. Sing   of   his   dy - ing   love,   Sing   of his   ris - ing   power:

Wake, ev - ery heart and ev - ery tongue, To praise the Sa-viour's name.
Sing how he in - ter-cedes a - bove For those whose sins he   bore.

3.
Soon shall we hear him say
Ye blessed children, come ;
Soon will he call us hence, away
To our eternal home.

4.
There shall each raptured tongue
His endless praise proclaim ;
And sweeter voices tune the song
Of Moses and the Lamb.

No. 228.

1
I LOVE thy kingdom, Lord,
   The house of thine abode,
The church our blest Redeemer saved
With his own precious blood.

2
I love thy church, O God,
   Her walls before thee stand,
Dear as the apple of thine eye,
And graven on thy hand.

3
For her my tears shall fall,
   For her my prayers ascend,
To her my cares and toils be given,
Till toils and cares shall end.

No. 229

1.
MY soul, repeat his praise,
   Whose mercies are so great,
Whose anger is so slow to rise,
   So ready to abate.

2.
His power subdues our sins,
   And his forgiving love,
Far as the east is from the west,
   Doth all our guilt remove.

3.
High as the heavens are raised
   Above the ground we tread,
So far the riches of his grace
   Our highest thoughts exceed.

No. 230   # Hebron. L.M.   Dr. L. Mason.

" Truly my soul waiteth upon God, from him cometh my salvation."

1. Je - sus, where'er thy peo-ple meet, There they be-hold thy mer - cy seat;

Where'er they seek thee, thou art found, And every place is hallow'd ground.

2	3
For thou within no walls confined, Dost dwell with those of humble mind ; Such ever bring thee where they come, And going, take thee to their home.	Great Shepherd of thy chosen few, Thy former mercies here renew ; Here to our waiting hearts, proclaim The sweetness of thy saving name.

No. 231

1

THUS far the Lord hath led me on—
Thus far his power prolongs my days;
And every evening shall make known
Some fresh memorial of his grace.

2

Much of my time has run to waste,
And I, perhaps, am near my home :
But he forgives my follies past,
And gives me strength for days to come.

3

Thus, when the night of death shall come,
My flesh shall rest beneath the ground,
And wait thy voice to rouse my tomb,
With sweet salvation in the sound.

No. 232

1

HOW blest the sacred tie that binds
In sweet communion kindred minds :
How swift the heavenly course they run,
Whose hearts, whose faith, whose hopes
are one.

2

To each, the soul of each how dear !
What tender love, what holy fear,
How does the generous flame within
Refine from earth, and cleanse from sin.

3

Nor shall the glowing flame expire,
When dimly burns frail nature's fire
Then shall they meet in realms above—
A heaven of joy—a heaven of love.

Ward. L.M.

No. 233   Arranged by Dr. Mason.

' And he shewed me a pure river of Water of Life."

1. There is a stream whose gen-tle flow Supplies the   ci - ty of   our God,
2. That sacred stream, thy ho-ly word, Supports our faith, our fears controls.

Life, love, and joy still gliding through, And wat'ring our di - vine a - bode.
Sweet peace thy pro-mis-es af - ford, And give new strength to fainting souls.

No. 234

1.

COME, let us tune our loftiest song,
   And raise to Christ our joyful strain;
Worship and thanks to him belong,
Who reigns, and shall for ever reign.

2.

His sovereign power our bodies made ;
Our souls are his immortal breath ;
And when his creatures sinn'd, he bled,
To save us from eternal death.

3.

Burn every breast with Jesus' love ;
Bound every heart with rapt'rous joy ;
And saints on earth, with saints above,
Your voices in his praise employ.

4.

Extol the Lamb with loftiest song,
Ascend for him our cheerful strain ;
Worship and thanks to him belong,
Who reigns, and shall for ever reign.

No. 235

1.

JUST as I am, without one plea,
   But that thy blood was shed for me,
And that thou bidst me come to thee,
O Lamb of God, I come, I come !

2.

Just as I am—poor, wretched, blind ;
Sight, riches, healing of the mind,
Yea, all I need in thee to find,
O Lamb of God, I come, I come !

3.

Just as I am, thou wilt receive,
Wilt welcome, pardon, cleanse, relieve !
Because thy promise I believe,
O Lamb of God, I come, I come !

4.

Just as I am—thy love unknown
Has broken every barrier down ;
Now to be thine, yea, thine alone,
O Lamb of God, I come, I come !

Greenville. 8's & 7's, Double.

No. 236   ROUSSEAU.

"O give thanks unto the Lord, for he is good : for his mercy endureth for ever."

1. Come,   thou   e - ver - last - ing   Spi - rit,   Bring   to   ev - ery
    All   the   Sav-iour's   dy - ing   me - rit,   All   his   suff - 'rings
D.C.   Now   re - veal his great sal - va - tion   Un - to   ev - ery

thank - ful   mind) True   re - cord - er   of   his   pas - sion,
for   man - kind :) Now   the   liv - ing   faith im - - - - - part.
faith - ful   heart.

2 Come, thou Witness of his dying ;   Let us groan thine inward groaning ;
   Come, Remembrancer divine ;   Look on him we pierced, and grieve ;
   Let us feel thy power applying   All partake the grace atoning ;
   Christ to every soul and mine :   All the sprinkled blood receive.

No. 237

LORD, dismiss us with thy blessing ;
   Fill our hearts with joy and peace ;
Let us each, thy love possessing,
   Triumph in redeeming grace ;
O refresh us, O refresh us,
   Travelling through this wilderness.
     O refresh us, etc.

2 Thanks we give, and adoration,
   For thy Gospel's joyful sound ;
May the fruits of thy salvation
   In our hearts and lives abound ;
May thy presence, may thy presence
   With us evermore be found.
     May thy presence, etc.

3 So, whene'er the signal's given,
   Us from earth to call away,
Borne on angels' wings to heaven,
   Glad the summons to obey,
May we ever, may we ever
   Reign with Christ in endless day.
     May we ever, etc.

No. 238

ZION stands with hills surrounded,
   Zion, kept by power divine :
All her foes shall be confounded,
   Though the world in arms combine :
Happy Zion, happy Zion,
   What a favour'd lot is thine !
     Happy Zion, etc.

2 Every human tie may perish ;
   Friend to friend unfaithful prove ;
Mothers cease their own to cherish ;
   Heaven and earth at last remove ;
But no changes, but no changes
   Can attend Jehovah's love.
     But no changes, etc.

3 In the furnace God may prove thee,
   Thence to bring thee forth more bright,
But can never cease to love thee ;
   Thou art precious in his sight :
God is with thee, God is with thee, —
   God, thine everlasting light.
     God is with thee, etc.

No. 239   **Dundee.** C.M.   GUIL. FRANC.

"In thy presence is fulness of joy."

1. Sin - ner, the voice of God re - gard; His mer - cy speaks to - day;
2. Like the rough sea that can - not rest, You live de - void of peace;

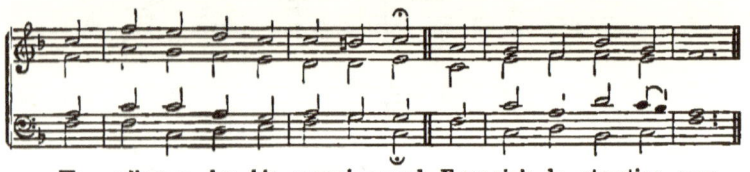

He   calls you by his sovereign word, From sin's de - structive way.
A   thousand stings with - in your breast De - prive your soul of ease.

No. 240

O, FOR a closer walk with God,
  A calm and heavenly frame,
A light to shine upon the road,
  That leads me to the Lamb!

2 Where is the blessedness I knew
  When first I saw the Lord?
Where is the soul-refreshing view
  Of Jesus and his word?

3 What peaceful hours I then enjoyed!
  How sweet their memory still!
But they have left an aching void,
  The world can never fill.

4 Return, O, holy Dove, return,
  Sweet messenger of rest;
I hate the sins that made thee mourn,
  And drove thee from my breast.

No. 241

O, FOR a faith that will not shrink,
  Though pressed by every foe,
That will not tremble on the brink
  Of any earthly woe;

2 That will not murmur nor complain
  Beneath the chastening rod,
But, in the hour of grief or pain,
  Will lean upon its God;—

3 A faith that keeps the narrow way
  Till life's last hour is fled,
And with a pure and heavenly ray
  Lights up a dying bed!

4 Lord, give us such a faith as this,
  And then, whate'er may come,
We'll taste, e'en here, the hallowed bliss
  Of an eternal home.

No. 242 **Retreat.** **L.M.** Dr. Hastings.

"O thou that hearest prayer, unto thee shall all flesh come."

1. From eve - ry stormy wind that blows, From every swelling tide of woes,

There is a calm, a sure retreat; 'Tis found beneath the mer - cy seat.

2.

There is a place where Jesus sheds
The oil of gladness on our heads;
A place than all besides more sweet, —
It is the blood-bought mercy-seat.

3.

There, there on eagles' wings we soar;
And sin and sense molest no more;
And heaven comes down our souls to greet,
While glory crowns the mercy-seat.

No. 243

1.

PRAYER is appointed to convey
The blessings God designs to give:
Long as they live should Christians pray;
They learn to pray when first they live.

2

If pain afflict, or wrongs oppress;
If cares distract, or fears dismay;
If guilt deject; if sin distress;
In every case, still watch and pray.

3.

'Tis prayer supports the soul that's
weak:
Though thought be broken, language
lame:
Pray, if thou canst or canst not speak;
But pray with faith in Jesus' name.

No. 244

1.

WHAT various hindrances we meet
In coming to a mercy-seat;
Yet who that knows the worth of prayer,
But wishes to be often there?

2.

Prayer makes the darken'd cloud with-
draw;
Prayer climbs the ladder Jacob saw;
Gives exercise to faith and love;
Brings every blessing from above.

3.

Restraining prayer, we cease to fight;
Prayer keeps the Christian's armour
bright;
And Satan trembles when he sees
The weakest saint upon his knees.

No. 245   ## Hamburg. L.M.   Dr. L. Mason.

" I will cry unto God most high : unto God that performeth all things for me."

1. Life is the time to serve the Lord, The time t'ensure the great re - ward ;

And while the lamp holds out to , burn, The vilest sin - ner may re - turn.

2.

Life is the hour that God hath given
T'escape from hell and fly to heaven ;
The day of grace ;—and mortals may
Secure the blessings of the day.

3.

There are no acts of pardon passed
In the cold grave to which we haste ;
But darkness, death, and long despair,
Reign in eternal silence there.

No. 246

1.

BEHOLD, a stranger's at the door !
He gently knocks—has knocked
before ;
Has waited long—is waiting still ;
You treat no other friend so ill.

2.

But will he prove a friend indeed ?
He will !—the very friend you need !
The Man of Nazareth !—'tis he,
With garments dyed at Calvary.

3.

Oh, lovely attitude !—he stands
With melting heart, and laden hands !
Oh ! matchless kindness ! — and he
shows
This matchless kindness to his foes.

4.

Admit him ere his anger burn—
His feet departed ne'er return ;
Admit him, or the hour's at hand
When at his door denied you'll stand !

No. 247

1.

SHOW pity, Lord ! O Lord, forgive !
Let a repenting rebel live.
Are not thy mercies large and free ?
May not a sinner trust in thee ?

2.

My crimes are great, but don't surpass
The power and glory of thy grace ;
Great God, thy nature hath no bound, —
So let thy pard'ning love be found.

3.

O wash my soul from every sin,
And make my guilty conscience clean ;
Here on my heart the burden lies,
And past offences pain my eyes.

4.

Yet save a trembling sinner, Lord,
Whose hope, still hov'ring round thy
word,
Would light on some sweet promise
there,--
Some sure support against despair.

Olmutz. s.m.

No. 248   Arranged by Dr. Mason.

"For he satisfieth the longing soul, and filleth the hungry soul with goodness."

1. Blest are the sons of peace, Whose hearts and hopes are one;

Whose kind designs to serve and please Through all their ac - tions run.

2.

Blest is the pious house,
Where zeal and friendship meet;
Their songs of praise, their mingled vows,
Make their communion sweet.

3.

Thus on the heavenly hills,
The saints are blest above,
When joy like morning dew distils,
And all the air is love.

No. 249

1.

HOW gentle God's commands!
How kind his precepts are!
Come, cast your burdens on the Lord,
And trust his constant care.

2.

Beneath his watchful eye
His saints securely dwell;
That hand which bears all nature up,
Shall guard his children well.

3.

Why should this anxious load
Press down your weary mind?
Haste to your heavenly Father's throne,
And sweet refreshment find.

No. 250

1.

ANOTHER day is past,
The hours for ever fled,
And time is bearing us away
To mingle with the dead.

2.

Our minds in perfect peace
Our Father's care shall keep;
We yield to gentle slumber now,
For thou canst never sleep.

3.

How blessed, Lord, are they
On thee securely stayed!
Nor shall they be in life alarmed,
Nor be in death dismayed.

No. 251   **Warwick.** c.m.   Stanley.

"Early in the morning will I direct my prayers unto thee."

1. Lord, in the morn-ing thou shalt hear My voice as-cend-ing high.

To thee will I di-rect my prayer,—To thee lift up mine eye :—

2.

Up to the hills where Christ is gone,
To plead for all his saints ;
Presenting, at the Father's throne,
Our songs and our complaints.

3.

O may thy Spirit guide my feet
In ways of righteousness,—
Make every path of duty straight
And plain before my face.

No. 252

1.

THERE is a land of pure delight,
Where saints immortal reign ;
Infinite day excludes the night,
And pleasures banish pain.

2.

There everlasting spring abides,
And never-with'ring flowers :
Death, like a narrow sea, divides
This heavenly land from ours.

3.

Sweet fields beyond the swelling flood
Stand dress'd in living green ;
So, to the Jews, old Canaan stood,
While Jordan roll'd between.

4.

Could we but climb where Moses stood,
And view the landscape o'er,
Not Jordan's stream, nor death's cold flood
Should fright us from the shore.

No. 253

1.

ONCE more we come before our God ;
Once more his blessing ask :
O may not duty seem a load,
Nor worship prove a task.

2.

Father, thy quick'ning spirit send
From heaven, in Jesus' name,
And bid our waiting minds attend,
And put our souls in frame.

3.

May we receive the word we hear,
Each in an honest heart ;
And keep the precious treasure there,
And never with it part.

4.

To seek thee, all our hearts dispose ;
To each thy blessing suit ;
And let the seed thy servant sows,
Produce abundant fruit.

No. 254   **Boylston.** S.M.   Dr. L. Mason.

" For this God is our God for ever and ever, he will be our guide even unto death."

1. Be - hold the throne of grace; The pro-mise calls us near;
2. Thine image, Lord, be - stow, Thy pre-sence and thy love,

There Je-sus shows a smi-ling face, And waits to an - swer prayer.
That we may serve thee here be - low, And reign with thee a - bove.

<table>
<tr><td>

3.

Teach us to live by faith,
Conform our wills to thine;
Let us victorious be in death,
And then in glory shine.

</td><td>

4.

If thou these blessings give,
And thou our portion be,
All worldly joys we'll gladly leave,
To find our heaven in thee.

</td></tr>
</table>

No. 255

1.

AND are we yet alive,
  And see each other's face ?
Glory and praise to Jesus give,
For his redeeming grace.

2.

Preserved by power divine
To full salvation here,
Again in Jesus' praise we join,
And in his sight appear.

3.

What troubles have we seen!
What conflicts have we pass'd!
Fightings without, and fears within,
Since we assembled last!

No. 256

1.

DID Christ o'er sinners weep,
  And shall our cheeks be dry ?
Let floods of penitential grief
Burst forth from every eye.

2.

The Son of God in tears
The wond'ring angels see ;
Be thou astonish'd, O my soul;
He shed those tears for thee.

3.

He wept that we might weep;
Each sin demands a tear:
In heaven alone no sin is found,
And there's no weeping there.

14

Martyn. 8 lines 7's.

No. 257   S. B. MARSH.

" He shall defend thee under his wings."

1. { Je - sus, lo - ver of my soul, Let me to thy bo - som fly, . . .
   { While the near-er wa - ters roll, While the tem-pest still is high ; . .
D C. Safe in - to the ha - ven guide, O re-ceive my soul at last. . .

Hide me, O my Sa-viour, hide,   Till the storm of life is past ;

2.	3.
Other refuge have I none ;	Plenteous grace with thee is found,
Hangs my helpless soul on thee :	Grace to cover all my sin :
Leave, O leave me not alone ;	Let the healing streams abound ;
Still support and comfort me ;	Make and keep me pure within.
All my trust on thee is stay'd ;	Thou of life the fountain art ;
All my help from thee I bring ;	Freely let me take of thee :
Cover my defenceless head	Spring thou up within my heart ;
With the shadow of thy wing.	Rise to all eternity

No. 258   **1.**

WHILE, with ceaseless course, the sun
     Hasted through the former year,
Many souls their race have run,
Never more to meet us here :
Fix'd in an eternal state,
They have done with all below :
We a little longer wait,
But how little, none can know.

2.

As the wingèd arrow flies,
Speedily the mark to find ;
As the lightning from the skies
Darts, and leaves no trace behind,—
Swiftly thus our fleeting days
Bear us down life's rapid stream ;
Upward, Lord, our spirits raise ;
All below is but a dream.

Rockingham. L.M.

Dr. L. Mason.

" Truly my soul waiteth upon God ; from Him cometh my salvation."

1. Far from my thoughts, vain world, begone, Let my re - li-gious hours alone;

Fain would mine eyes my Saviour see ;   I   wait   a   vi - sit, Lord, from thee.

2	3.
O warm my heart with holy fire,	Hail, great Immanuel, all divine!
And kindle there a pure desire :	In thee thy Father's glories shine ;
Come, sacred Spirit, from above,	Thy glorious name shall be adored,
And fill my soul with heavenly love.	And every tongue confess thee Lord.

No. 260
1.

MY Father, when I come to thee,
   I would not only bend the knee,
But with my spirit seek thy face,—
With my whole heart desire thy grace.

2.

My Saviour, guide me with thine eye;
My sins forgive, my wants supply ;
With favour crown my youthful days,
And my whole life shall speak thy praise.

3.

Thy Holy Spirit, Lord, impart ;
Impress thy likeness on my heart ;
May I obey thy truth in love,
Till raised to dwell with thee above.

No 261
1.

GREAT God, behold, before thy throne
   A band of children lowly bend ;
Thy face we seek, thy name we own,
And pray that thou wilt be our Friend.

2.

Thy Holy Spirit's aid impart,
That he may teach us how to pray ;
Make us sincere, and let each heart
Delight to tread in wisdom's way.

3.

O let thy grace our souls renew,
And seal a sense of pardon there ;
Teach us thy will to know and do,
And let us all thine image bear.

No. 262   # Evan.   C.M.   OLD SCOTCH MELODY.

" Thou shalt not be afraid for the terror by night."

1. In mer-cy, Lord, re-mem-ber me, Through all the hours of night,

And grant to me most gra-cious-ly The safe-guard of thy might.

2.

With cheerful heart I close mine eyes,
Since thou wilt not remove :
O, in the morning let me rise
Rejoicing in thy love.

3.

Or, if this night should prove my last,
And end my transient days ;
Lord, take me to thy promised rest,
Where I may sing thy praise.

No. 263

1.

COME, Holy Spirit, heavenly Dove,
With all thy quick'ning powers ;
Kindle a flame of sacred love
In these cold hearts of ours.

2.

In vain we tune our formal songs,—
In vain we strive to rise ;
Hosannas languish on our tongues,
And our devotion dies.

3.

Father, and shall we ever live
At this poor dying rate ;
Our love so faint, so cold to thee,
And thine to us so great ?

4.

Come, Holy Spirit, heavenly Dove,
With all thy quick'ning powers ;
Come, shed abroad a Saviour's love,
And that shall kindle ours.

No. 264

1.

COME, ye that love the Saviour's name,
And joy to make it known ;
The Sov'reign of your hearts proclaim,
And bow before his throne.

2.

Behold your Lord, your Master, crown'd
With glories all divine,
And tell the wond'ring nations round,
How bright those glories shine.

3.

When, in his earthly courts, we view
The glories of our King,
We long to love as angels do,
And wish, like them, to sing.

4.

And shall we long and wish in vain ?
Lord, teach our songs to rise :
Thy love can animate the strain,
And bid it reach the skies.

Jesus, our Shepherd. s.m.

No. 265

J. ZUNDEL.

"My sheep hear my voice."

1. I was a wand'ring sheep, I did not love the fold ; I did not love my

Shepherd's voice, I would not be con-troll'd ; I was a wayward child, I

did not love my home; I did not love my Father's voice, I loved a-far to roam.

2.	3.
The Shepherd sought his sheep,	Jesus my Shepherd is,
The Father sought his child ;	'Twas he that loved my soul,
They followed me o'er vale and hill,	'Twas he that washed me in his blood,
O'er deserts waste and wild :	'Twas he that made me whole :
They found me nigh to death,	'Twas he that sought the lost,
Famish'd, and faint, and lone ;	That found the wandering sheep,
They bound me with the bands of love,	'Twas he that brought me to the fold—
They saved the wandering one.	'Tis he that still doth keep.

No. 266

1	2.
THE Lord my Shepherd is,	If e'er I go astray,
I shall be well supplied ;	He doth my soul reclaim ;
Since he is mine, and I am his,	And guides me in his own right way,
What can I want beside ?	For his most holy name.
He leads me to the place	While he affords his aid,
Where heavenly pasture grows,	I cannot yield to fear, [dark shade,
Where living waters gently pass,	Though I should walk through death's
And full salvation flows.	My Shepherd's with me there.

With the Lord.

No. 267.

I. B. WOODBURY.

So shall we ever be with the Lord."

1. For ev - er with the Lord, A - men, so let it be; Life from the dead is in that word, 'Tis im - mor - tal - i - ty. Here in the bod - y pent, Ab - sent from him I roam; Yet night - ly pitch my mov - ing tent A day's march near - er home; Near - er home, near - er home, A day's march near - er home.

2 My Father's house on high,
  Home of my soul, how near
At times, to Faith's foreseeing eye,
  Thy golden gates appear.—*Here in, &c.*

3 My thirsty spirit faints
  To reach the land I love,

The bright inheritance of saints,
  Jerusalem above.—*Here in, &c.*

4 For ever with the Lord!
  Father, if 'tis thy will,
The promise of that faithful word
  Ev'n here to me fulfil.—*Here in, &c.*

No. 268.

1 SOLDIERS of Christ, arise!
  And put your armor on;
Strong in the strength which God supplies
  Through his eternal Son.
Strong in the Lord of Hosts,
  And in his mighty power,
Who in the strength of Jesus trusts,
  Is more than conqueror.

2 Leave no unguarded place,—
  No weakness of the soul;
Take every virtue, every grace,
  And fortify the whole.
Indissolubly joined,
  To battle all proceed;
But arm yourselves with all the mind
  That was in Christ, your Head.

Onward, Christians!

No. 269

Württemberg Melody.

" In everything give thanks."

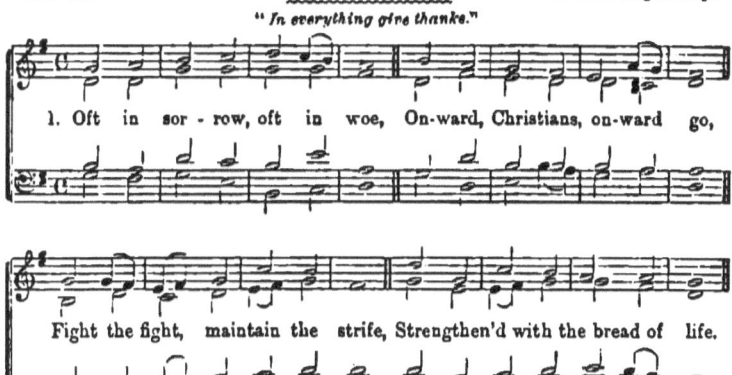

1. Oft in sor - row, oft in woe, On-ward, Christians, on-ward go,

Fight the fight, maintain the strife, Strengthen'd with the bread of life.

2.

Onward, Christians, onward go,
Join the war and face the foe;
Will ye flee in danger's hour?
Know ye not your Captain's power?

3.

Onward then in battle move;
More than conqueror's ye shall prove;
Though opposed by many a foe,
Christian soldiers, onward go!

Graces.

No. 270
OLD HUNDREDTH. L.M.

BEFORE MEAT.
See page 193.

B E present at our table, Lord,
Be here and everywhere adored;
These mercies bless, and grant that we
May feast in Paradise with thee.

No. 271
SESSIONS. L.M.

AFTER MEAT.
See page 93.

W E thank thee, Lord, for this our food;
But most of all for Jesu's blood:
Let manna to our souls be given,
The bread of life sent down from heaven.

No. 272

Bright Home.*

Arr. by Phillips.

"In my father's house are many mansions."

1. Bright home of our Saviour, what glo - ries a - wait The spir - its that pass thro' thy bright pearly gate; What an - thems of rap - ture, un - ceas - ing and high, Com - pose the loud cho - rus that glad - dens the sky? Home, home, sweet, sweet home; Pre - pare me, dear Sav - iour, for yon - der blest home.

2 The home of the ransom'd, the land of the blest;
Where pilgrims shall enter a glorious rest;
Shall wander in gladness the pastures of green,
And drink the still waters of pleasures serene.

3 The home that our Saviour has gone to prepare—
No heart can conceive of the blessedness there,
Of raptures unending awaiting the just,
When pure in his likeness they rise from the dust.

4 We bless thee, dear Saviour, who call'st us to share
The beautiful home thou hast gone to prepare;
We trust in thy mercy, that, wash'd from our sin,
Through yonder bright gates we may all enter in.

* Air—*home, sweet home.*

Closing Day. S.M.

No. 273

REV. A. E. LORD.

" As for man, his days are as grass."

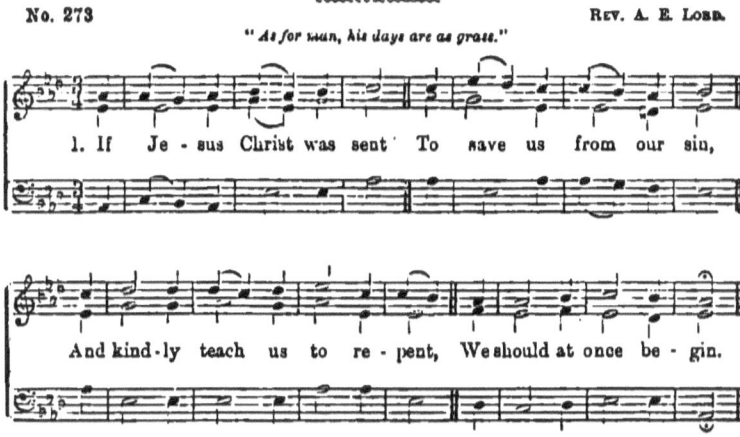

1. If Je - sus Christ was sent ' To save us from our sin,
And kind - ly teach us to re - pent, We should at once be - gin.

2.

'Tis not enough to say
We're sorry and repent,
Yet still go on, from day to day,
Just as we always went.

3.

Repentance, is to leave
The sins we loved before,
And show that we in earnest grieve,
By doing so no more.

4.

Lord, make us thus sincere,
To watch as well as pray ;
However small, however dear,
Take all our sins away.

5.

And since the Saviour came,
To make us turn from sin,
With holy grief and humble shame,
May we at once begin.

No. 274

1.

THE day is past and gone ;
The evening shades appear ;
Oh may we all remember well,
The night of death draws near.

2.

We lay our garments by,
Upon our beds to rest ;
So death shall soon disrobe us all
Of what we here possessed.

3.

Lord, keep us safe this night,
Secure from all our fears ;
May angels guard us while we sleep,
Till morning light appears.

4.

And when our days are past,
And we from time remove,
Lord, may we in thy bosom rest,
The bosom of thy love.

No. 275   # Coronation. C.M.   OLIVER HOLDEN.

"All the earth shall be filled with His majesty."

1. All hail the power of Je - sus' name, Let an - gels prostrate fall;

Bring forth the roy - al di - a - dem, And crown him Lord of all.

Bring forth the roy - al di - a - dem, And crown him Lord of all.

2 Let every kindred, every tribe
  On this terrestrial ball
To him all majesty ascribe,
  And crown him Lord of all.
        To him, etc.

3 O that with yonder sacred throng
  We at his feet may fall!
We'll join the everlasting song,
  And crown him Lord of all.
        We'll join, etc.

No. 276

O FOR a thousand tongues to sing
  My great Redeemer's praise ;
The glories of my God and King,
  The triumphs of his grace !
        The glories of, etc.

2 My gracious Master, and my God,
  Assist me to proclaim,—
To spread through all the earth abroad
  The honours of thy Name.
        To spread, etc.

3 Jesus!—the Name that charms our fears,
  That bids our sorrows cease ;
'Tis music in the sinner's ears,
  'Tis life, and health, and peace.
        'Tis music, etc.

No. 277

COME, let us join our cheerful songs,
  With angels round the throne :
Ten thousand thousand are their tongues,
  But all their joys are one.
        Ten thousand, etc.

2 Jesus is worthy to receive
  Honour and power divine ;
And blessings more than we can give,
  Be, Lord, for ever thine.
        And blessings, etc.

3 The whole creation join in one,
  To bless the sacred name
Of Him that sits upon the throne,
  And to adore the Lamb.
        Of Him, etc.

Both Sides the River.

"For now we see through a glass darkly, but then face to face."

No. 278

Philip Phillips.

1. Life is but a fleet-ing dream, Ou - ly strangers here we roam;

Life is but a changeful scene, Yon-der is the Christian's home.

Just be-yond the roll - ing tide An - gels watch us on the shore,

Where the pearl-y wa - ters glide, And the wea - ry thirst no more.

2 Here we feel the tempter's power,
Here we sigh for living-bread,
Clouds of gloom and darkness lower,
While a rugged path we tread.
There no cruel thorns are found,
Doubt and fear and storms are o'er,
There the fruits of joy abound,
We shall hunger there no more.

3 Here we breathe the sultry air
Of a lonely desert plain,
Tria's here the heart must bear
Worn by sickness, racked with pain.

There the waves of death are passed,
There, among the pure and blest,
Safely anchored home at last,
There our wandering feet shall rest.

4 Here our fondest hopes are brief,
Kindred ties are broken here;
Morn'ng brings a night of grief,
Joy is mingled with a tear.
There shall faith be lost in sight,
There a long eternal day.
Christ the Lamb shall be the Light,
He will wipe our tears away.

Cleansing Fountain. C. M.

No. 279

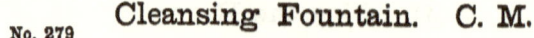

1. There is a fountain filled with blood, Drawn from Im - man-uel's veins,

And sin - ners plunged beneath that flood, Lose all their guilt - y stains;

Lose all their guilt - y stains, Lose all their guilt - y stains;

And sin - ners plunged beneath that flood, Lose all their guilt - y stains.

2 The dying thief rejoiced to see
That fountain in his day ;
And there may I, though vile as he,
Wash all my sins away.

3 E'er since by faith I saw the stream
Thy flowing wounds supply,
Redeeming love has been my theme,
And shall be till I die.

4 Then in a nobler, sweeter song
I'll sing thy power to save,
When this poor, lisping, stammering tongue,
Lies silent in the grave.

No. 280.

1 LET worldly minds the world pursue;
It has no charms for me :
Once I admired its trifles too,
But grace hath set me free.

2 As by the light of opening day
The stars are all concealed,
So earthly pleasures fade away,
When Jesus is revealed.

4 Creatures no more divide my choice ;
I bid them all depart :
His name, his love, his gracious voice,
Have fixed my roving heart.

Familiar Hymns.

No. 281.   "*Bethany*," Key G.

1 NEARER, my God, to thee,
Nearer to thee!
E'en though it be a cross
That raiseth me,
Still all my song shall be,
Nearer, my God, to thee,
Nearer to thee!

2 Though like a wanderer,
The sun gone down,
Darkness comes over me,
My rest a stone,
Yet in my dreams I'd be, Nearer, etc.

3 There let my way appear
Steps unto heaven;
All that thou sendest me,
In mercy given;
Angels to beckon me, Nearer, etc.

4 Or, if on joyful wing,
Cleaving the sky,
Sun, moon, and stars forgot,
Upward I fly,
Still all my song shall be, Nearer, etc.

No. 282.   "*Oak*," Key G.

1 I'M but a stranger here,
Heaven is my home;
Earth is a desert drear,
Heaven is my home,
Danger and sorrow stand
Round me on every hand;
Heaven is my fatherland,
Heaven is my home.

2 What though the tempest rage,
Heaven is my home;
Short is my pilgrimage,
Heaven is my home.
Time's cold and wintry blast
Soon will be overpast;
I shall reach home at last,
Heaven is my home.

3 There at my Saviour's side,
Heaven is my home,
I shall be glorified,
Heaven is my home.
There are the good and blest,
Those I loved most and best,
There, too, I soon shall rest,
Heaven is my home.

No. 283.   "*Boylston*," Key C.

1 Sow in the morn thy seed;
At eve hold not thy hand;
To doubt and fear give thou no heed,
Broadcast it o'er the land.

2 Thou know'st not which shall thrive,
The late or early sown;
Grace keeps the precious germ alive,
When and wherever strewn.

3 Thou canst not toil in vain;
Cold, heat, and moist, and dry,
Shall foster and mature the grain
For garners in the sky.

No. 284.   "*Gather at the River*," Key Eb.

SHALL we gather at the river,
Where bright angel feet have trod?
With its crystal tide forever
Flowing by the throne of God?

CHO. Yes, we'll gather at the river,
The beautiful, the beautiful river;
Gather with the saints at the river,
That flows by the throne of God.

2 On the margin of the river,
Washing up its silver spray,
We will walk and worship ever,
All the happy, golden day.—CHO.

3 Ere we reach the shining river,
Lay we every burden down;
Grace our spirit will deliver,
And provide a robe and crown.—CHO.

4 Soon we'll reach the silver river,
Soon our pilgrimage will cease;
Soon our happy hearts will quiver
With the melody of peace.—CHO.

No. 285.   "*Shining Shore*," Key G.

1 My days are gliding swiftly by,
And I, a pilgrim stranger,
Would not detain them as they fly,
These hours of toil and danger.

CHO. For now we stand on Jordan's strand,
Our friends are passing over;
And just before the shining shore
We may almost discover.

2 We'll gird our loins, my brethren
dear,
Our heavenly home discerning;
Our absent Lord has left us word,
Let every lamp be burning.—CHO.

3 Let sorrow's rudest tempest blow,
Each cord on earth to sever,
Our king says come, and there's our
home,
Forever, oh, forever!—CHO.

INDEX OF TUNES.

INDEX OF FIRST LINES.